THE RESONANT MARKETS SERIES

The Markets Hidden Frequency

How Emotional Energy, Collective Behavior, and Flow Shape Price Moves

Deepanshu Suman

2025 First Edition

Copyright

Title: The Market's Hidden Frequency
Author: Deepanshu Suman

First Edition
ISBN: 978-93-344-5119-1

Disclaimer: This book is intended for educational and reflective purposes. It explores psychological, conceptual, and behavioral frameworks for understanding market dynamics and decision-making. The material presented does not constitute financial, investment, or trading advice. Readers are encouraged to exercise independent judgment and consult qualified professionals before applying any concepts or interpretations from this work.

Dedication

For the observers, feelers, and seekers
who sense the pulse beneath the chart,
who listen to the rhythm between price and perception,
and who understand that every move
is a mirror of collective emotion.

This book is for those who trade not just with logic,
but with awareness
who seek coherence between mind and market,
and who find harmony in uncertainty.

Acknowledgments

Writing this book was both a reflection and a resonance a dialogue with the unseen forces that move markets and minds alike. My heartfelt gratitude to the readers, thinkers, and traders who resonated with the first book and inspired this deeper exploration. To every curious soul who questions patterns, emotions, and meaning in the flow of price this work exists because you listen where others only look. And to those building coherence in a world of noise may your awareness always stay tuned to truth, balance, and flow.

Preface

Why This Book Exists

Markets are not merely systems of numbers and charts—they are living, breathing entities reflecting human emotion, cognition, and collective energy. Beneath every price movement lies a rhythm of fear and greed, clarity and confusion, impulse and insight. This book exists to decode those unseen frequencies—to help traders recognize that markets mirror the mind itself.

Positioning Within the Series

This volume is part of *The Resonant Markets Series*, an exploration of how human consciousness interacts with market systems. While the first book examined awareness, perception, and the psychological foundations of market behavior, this book moves deeper—into resonance, alignment, and the energetic feedback loops that govern collective decision-making. It bridges quantitative logic with qualitative intuition, creating a unified framework for understanding the emotional structure of markets.

What Readers Will Gain

Readers will learn to perceive markets not as chaotic forces, but as coherent energetic fields that can be read, felt, and aligned with. Through **conceptual frameworks**, **behavioral insights**, and **mental calibration tools**, this book helps traders refine their inner state—improving both perception and execution. Exercises throughout the book train emotional neutrality, cognitive precision, and resonance-based decision-making, guiding readers toward mastery of both mind and market.

Purpose & Unique Proposition

- **Core Insight:** Markets function as *living, resonant systems*, not mechanical constructs.

- **Approach:** Blends *psychology*, *behavioral finance*, and *conceptual systems thinking* to develop aligned decision-making.
- **Outcome:** Practical *mental models* and *perceptual exercises* for traders to synchronize thought, emotion, and action.

Target Audience

- Advanced retail and professional traders seeking to understand the psychological and emotional architecture behind price movements.
- Reflective thinkers drawn to the intersection of market structure, behavior, and consciousness.
- Returning readers from the first book who wish to go deeper—into the collective mind and emotional field that shapes every market wave.

Introduction

Markets as Living, Resonant Systems

The market is not a machine. It is a field alive, dynamic, and responsive to human consciousness. Every candle on a chart, every surge in volume, every phase of volatility is an echo of collective emotion and belief. Behind the quantitative surface of prices lies a vast energetic network where perception, expectation, and attention interact to create resonance.

In this sense, the market behaves less like a predictable algorithm and more like an organism adapting, learning, self-correcting. It mirrors the state of its participants, amplifying confidence or fear depending on what frequency dominates the collective psyche. Those who learn to feel this rhythm, to sense alignment between signal and sentiment, begin to trade not against the market but with it.

This book explores that living structure: how thought becomes movement, how emotion becomes volatility, and how alignment between inner state and external flow defines true mastery.

Beyond Standard Trading Books

Most trading books teach indicators, systems, or strategies tools that promise clarity in the chaos. But few address the underlying pattern that drives all patterns: the human mind.

Technical setups are only shadows of psychological states. Indicators lag because emotion moves first. To truly understand markets, one must study the underlying resonance between cognition, emotion, and crowd behavior.

This book moves beyond surface mechanics to reveal the invisible architecture of movement how awareness, attention, and alignment create market structure. It is less about "what to trade" and more about "how to perceive." You will not find formulas to memorize or systems to copy only frameworks to evolve your thinking, and calibration tools to refine your intuition.

The aim is not to trade mechanically, but consciously.

How to Read and Use This Book

This book is both a mirror and a map. Each chapter invites you to pause, reflect, and experiment. It is designed not for passive reading but for active calibration of your perception, attention, and decision-making process.

- **Reflective Exercises:** Each section includes guided reflections to help you recognize your own emotional and cognitive patterns in trading. Take time to journal your insights awareness compounds through observation.
- **Mental Calibration:** Think of the book as a training field for clarity. The goal is to synchronize thought and action to act from alignment, not reaction.
- **Applied Practice:** You'll be invited to apply concepts directly to live or simulated trading environments. The purpose is to bridge insight with execution transforming understanding into embodied skill.

The chapters are nonlinear by design you may move freely between them, revisiting concepts as your awareness deepens. Each idea is part of a larger resonance a field of thought that evolves as you engage with it.

This is not a manual to be completed; it is a conversation to be lived. If you allow the process, the market will begin to reflect your internal clarity and alignment will replace anxiety as your trading edge.

"The market reveals what the mind projects. To master one is to understand the other."

Contents

Part I

Markets as Living Resonant Systems

Chapter 1

The Pulse Beneath the Chart

Before the chart, before the numbers, there is rhythm.

Every market carries a hidden pulse a pattern of acceleration and pause, expansion and contraction like the heartbeat of a living organism. What most traders call "price action" is merely the visible skin of something deeper: a collective nervous system transmitting the emotion of millions.

Every candle is a breath. Every trend is a heartbeat. And every reversal is a shift in mood the silent pivot when optimism turns to hesitation, or fear gives way to curiosity again. Beneath every move lies energy not just capital, but attention, belief, and emotion flowing through the system.

Traders often look for patterns in data, but the deeper game is to feel patterns in emotion. When fear floods, liquidity dries. When euphoria peaks, energy disperses. The market, like any biological system, seeks equilibrium but only after the emotional waves have fully expressed themselves.

This chapter explores that living rhythm how emotion becomes structure, how price embodies energy, and how collective psychology forms the unseen infrastructure of movement. Once you begin to feel the pulse beneath the chart, you stop reacting to randomness and start listening to resonance.

The goal is not to predict, but to perceive.

1.1 Markets as Emotional Organisms

Markets are more than numbers on a screen or trends on a chart. They are **living systems**, composed of interconnected minds, emotions, and decisions, constantly interacting across time and space. Every market move is the product of countless micro-decisions, each reflecting the beliefs, fears, hopes, and impulses of participants. Viewed collectively, these interactions resemble the behavior of a complex organism responsive, adaptive, and inherently emotional.

The Biological Analogy

Consider a biological organism: it senses its environment, reacts to stimuli, and self-regulates to maintain equilibrium. Markets operate similarly. News, events, and rumors are stimuli entering the system. Traders, investors, and institutions respond emotionally and cognitively, creating feedback loops that amplify or dampen price movements. Like a heart beating in response to external or internal triggers, markets pulse with collective sentiment. Periods of calm reflect equilibrium, while volatility signals emotional tension and energetic shifts.

Emotion as the Driving Force

Traditional finance models often assume rational actors, but decades of behavioral research show that **emotion dominates decision-making**. Fear, greed, hope, despair, and excitement manifest not only in trading behavior but also in observable market patterns:

- **Fear** contracts liquidity, causing sudden sell-offs or panic movements.
- **Greed** expands activity, inflating trends beyond logical valuation.
- **Hope** sustains gradual accumulation or buying during consolidation.
- **Despair** leads to capitulation, resetting market expectations.

These emotional states create what can be called the **emotional anatomy** of the market: the underlying structure of impulses that informs visible price action. In essence, **price is the expression of emotion**, while volume and volatility are its energy signature.

The Collective Nervous System

Markets function like a distributed nervous system. Information flows rapidly across participants, creating near-instantaneous reactions. Rumors, analyst reports, social media sentiment, or central bank announcements act as stimuli. Each trader's perception contributes to the global feedback loop, reinforcing or attenuating trends.

This network is **self-organizing**: no single actor controls the pulse, yet the system exhibits coherence. When a critical mass of participants aligns emotionally, movements accelerate. When discord dominates, indecision slows the market. Understanding this "collective nervous system" allows traders to anticipate not only movements but also the emotional tension behind them.

Recognizing Emotional Micro-Signals

Emotional micro-signals are subtle precursors of market moves. They may include:

- Shifts in order flow or trade size
- Subtle sentiment changes in news and social platforms
- Rapid changes in implied volatility or option pricing
- Patterns of hesitation or acceleration in price movement

Traders attuned to these signals can detect **early resonance**, where small inputs create disproportionately large outcomes much like neural firing in an organism.

Practical Implications for Traders

Seeing markets as emotional organisms changes how one trades:

1. **Shift from prediction to perception:** Focus on sensing emotional waves, rather than mechanically forecasting prices.
2. **Develop awareness of feedback loops:** Recognize when collective sentiment is amplifying or damping moves.
3. **Tune to the pulse:** Observe subtle cues volatility, volume spikes, sentiment shifts as indicators of underlying energy.
4. **Align actions with resonance:** Trade in harmony with the market's emotional rhythm, rather than against it.

In this framework, **mastery is not control, but connection**. The most successful traders are those who understand that markets reflect the human mind en masse and who learn to move in sync with this living, emotional system.

"To understand the market, you must listen not to its prices, but to its pulse."

1.2 Price as Energy Transfer

Price is more than a numeric value; it is the **visible expression of invisible energy** flowing through the market. Every trade, every order, every change in sentiment represents a transfer of attention, belief, and intention. Understanding price as energy allows traders to see movement not as arbitrary, but as the result of cumulative human and institutional dynamics.

The Market as an Energy Field

Imagine the market as a fluid energy field. Buyers inject energy into the system through conviction, desire, and risk-taking. Sellers withdraw energy through caution, hesitation, or capitulation. The resulting price movement is the net effect of these opposing flows, oscillating like waves across the market landscape.

- **Momentum:** High conviction from a critical mass of participants creates concentrated energy that propels prices.
- **Resistance:** Price levels where opposing energy accumulates can absorb movement, creating tension before release.
- **Volatility:** Sudden shifts in collective energy cause rapid oscillations, signaling disequilibrium or emotional turbulence.

Every price change is thus an **energy transaction**, not merely a reflection of value. Understanding this allows traders to sense the **flow of capital and sentiment**, rather than only observing historical price data.

Energy Transfer in Micro-Moments

Even small trades can carry measurable energy. Micro-moments a rapid buy-sell imbalance, an unexpected spike in volume, or a subtle order book shift are micro-transfers of emotional and cognitive energy.

Over time, these micro-moments aggregate into larger trends, much like small electrical impulses summing to produce a nerve signal. By observing energy transfer at multiple scales, traders can detect **early resonance** and anticipate potential expansions or contractions in the market.

Psychology and Energy Flow

Energy is not purely mechanical; it is deeply psychological. Fear, greed, hope, and doubt act as sources and sinks of market energy:

- **Fear** withdraws energy, compressing price movement and increasing tension.
- **Greed** injects energy, amplifying momentum and extending trends.

- **Hope and Uncertainty** create oscillations, often causing sideways or choppy markets.

Price, then, is a **thermometer of collective emotion**, translating internal states into observable market activity.

Energy and Market Mechanics

Conceptualizing price as energy transfer reframes common trading concepts:

- **Support and Resistance:** Points of energy accumulation where the market absorbs or releases emotional intensity.
- **Breakouts:** Sudden energy surges overcoming accumulated resistance.
- **Reversals:** Energy shifts from one dominant force to another, often signaled by micro-signal exhaustion or new input.

Volume, volatility, and order flow become **proxies for energy levels**, helping traders quantify emotional intensity without reducing the market to mere numbers.

Practical Implications for Traders

Viewing price as energy transfer shifts the trader's role from analyst to observer of energetic dynamics:

1. **Sense Flow Before Reaction:** Recognize the buildup or depletion of energy before making a trade.
2. **Follow the Path of Least Resistance:** Align trades with dominant energy flow, rather than fighting against it.
3. **Detect Early Resonance:** Micro-moments often precede large-scale price moves; attention to subtle energy shifts improves timing.
4. **Calibrate Emotional Alignment:** Maintain internal energy coherence to avoid being swept by collective overreaction.

By treating price as the **manifestation of emotional and cognitive energy**, traders gain a deeper, more intuitive understanding of market mechanics. It is no longer just about levels, patterns, or indicators it is about **reading the flow of human attention, belief, and intent** across the entire market organism.

"Price is not a number; it is the echo of millions of minds in motion."

1.3 The Collective Nervous System of Markets

Markets do not operate as isolated individuals making independent decisions. They function as a **distributed, interconnected nervous system**, where the thoughts, emotions, and actions of each participant ripple through the system, influencing all others. Just as neurons communicate through electrochemical signals, traders transmit energy through decisions, orders, and sentiment creating a dynamic network of cause and effect.

The Anatomy of Market Communication

At its core, the market is a communication network. Price movements, trade volume, news, social media, and rumors act as **signals** traveling through the system. Each participant perceives, interprets, and reacts to these signals, feeding back into the network and altering the state of the market.

This feedback loop creates emergent behavior: patterns and trends arise not from a single actor, but from the **collective processing of information and emotion**. The market's "intelligence" is therefore **distributed**, adaptive, and constantly evolving.

Feedback Loops and Amplification

The collective nervous system thrives on feedback:

- **Positive Feedback Loops:** When optimism spreads, buying begets more buying. Rising prices attract attention, which generates further energy injection, amplifying the move.
- **Negative Feedback Loops:** When prices rise too fast, fear of loss triggers selling, draining energy and restoring equilibrium.

These loops are the mechanism by which small inputs micro-signals, individual trades, or subtle shifts in sentiment can **cascade into large-scale market movements**. Understanding these loops allows traders to identify **points of amplification or attenuation**, where a minor emotional impulse can lead to significant price impact.

Networked Cognition and Collective Psychology

Each trader is a node in the system, but nodes are **psychologically entangled**:

- Institutional behavior informs retail sentiment, and vice versa.
- Media narratives shape expectations, altering the flow of energy through perception.

- Herding behavior arises when nodes align emotionally, creating synchronized movement.

This creates a **psychological resonance** across the market shared beliefs, fears, or hopes reverberate through multiple assets and timeframes simultaneously. In essence, the market "feels" as one organism, even though it is composed of millions of independent minds.

Signals, Noise, and Nervous System Sensitivity

Not all information is meaningful. The market transmits a mixture of **signals and noise**, just as a biological nervous system distinguishes between vital sensory input and background static. Traders who attune to the system's energy can identify **true signals** shifts in collective sentiment versus superficial movements or random fluctuations.

Key indicators of the nervous system's state include:

- Rapid accumulation or withdrawal of positions
- Sudden spikes in implied volatility
- Correlated movement across related assets
- Repetition of emotional micro-patterns in price and volume

The more sensitive a trader becomes to these cues, the earlier they can **anticipate resonance events**, where the market's collective nervous system is about to release or absorb energy.

Practical Implications for Traders

Recognizing the market as a collective nervous system transforms strategy:

1. **Observe Interconnections:** Track not just a single asset, but the network of influences and related markets.
2. **Detect Tension Points:** Identify where collective sentiment is building pressure that may soon be released.
3. **Align with Systemic Flow:** Avoid fighting the dominant energy propagation; trade with, not against, emergent patterns.
4. **Use Multi-Scale Awareness:** Consider both micro-level impulses and macro-level waves to anticipate cascading movements.

By treating markets as **living, nervous networks**, traders move from reactive behavior to **resonant observation**, sensing not just what is happening, but how the system is feeling and preparing to respond.

"The market does not act alone; it speaks through the minds and hearts of all who participate."

1.4 Recognizing Emotional Micro-Signals

If markets are living organisms, then emotional micro-signals are their subtle heartbeats and nerve impulses. These are the **tiny, often invisible cues** that precede larger movements micro-expressions of collective sentiment that, if observed carefully, reveal the underlying energy and direction of the market.

Defining Micro-Signals

Emotional micro-signals are **small-scale indicators of collective psychology**, embedded in price action, volume patterns, order flow, and market behavior. They are not the obvious trends or breakouts; they are the subtle tremors that hint at the organism's next movement.

Some examples include:

- **Small but sudden shifts in order size or bid-ask imbalance**: Indicating tentative movement from cautious participants.
- **Rapid, shallow spikes in volatility**: Often a precursor to accumulation or distribution before larger trends.
- **Mini reversals or rejections at key levels**: Suggesting hesitation or internal conflict within the market's collective sentiment.
- **Clusters of correlated micro-movements across related assets**: Revealing emergent alignment or tension within the network.

These micro-signals are analogous to **subtle emotional expressions in humans**: a twitch, a pause, a breath. Individually, they may seem insignificant, but when aggregated, they form the **early signs of resonance and market momentum.**

Psychological Basis of Micro-Signals

Micro-signals arise from the **emotional and cognitive states of participants**:

- **Fear** generates hesitation: small pullbacks, shallow retracements, and reduced order size.
- **Greed** creates impulsive bursts: rapid price spikes, sudden volume surges, or aggressive positioning.
- **Uncertainty** produces oscillations: choppy price action, indecision at key levels, and increased testing of support or resistance.

By observing these patterns, traders can detect **latent tension** before it becomes visible as a trend, correction, or breakout. This is analogous to sensing micro-expressions in social interactions small cues reveal the internal state before overt behavior manifests.

Micro-Signals in Price and Volume

Price and volume are the primary conduits of emotional energy.

- **Price micro-signals**: rapid, subtle movements around support and resistance, failed breakouts, or temporary overshoots.
- **Volume micro-signals**: small spikes indicating the entry or exit of cautious participants, often preceding larger accumulation or distribution.

Recognizing the **relationship between price and volume micro-signals** provides a real-time window into market sentiment and energetic balance.

Integration Across Timeframes

Micro-signals are scale-independent: they appear in intraday charts, daily candles, or even weekly patterns. The key is **contextual awareness**:

- Confirm whether a micro-signal aligns with broader market energy.
- Observe repeated micro-patterns across multiple timeframes these often indicate **emerging resonance**.
- Distinguish isolated noise from coordinated emotional response.

Practical Steps for Traders

1. **Observe Before Acting:** Pause and note micro-signals as they emerge, without immediately entering trades. 2. **Maintain Emotional Neutrality:** Avoid projecting personal bias onto small movements; let the signals speak for the market. 3. **Aggregate Observations:** Look for clusters of micro-signals across assets, timeframes, and order flows. 4. **Anticipate Resonance:** Use micro-signals to position ahead of larger energy releases, not to force trades prematurely. 5. **Journal Observations:** Record patterns of micro-signals and outcomes; this trains perceptual sensitivity over time.

Conclusion

Emotional micro-signals are the **early whispers of the market's collective mind**. They allow perceptive traders to sense tension, alignment, and emerging movement before it manifests as overt price action. By cultivating awareness of these subtle cues, traders move from reaction to resonance from observing numbers to **listening to the living pulse beneath the chart**.

"The smallest tremors often herald the largest waves. Learn to hear the market's whispers."

1.5 Case Examples: Historical and Recent Markets

Theory becomes meaningful when grounded in observation. Markets, as living organisms, reveal their emotional and energetic rhythms most clearly through historical and recent examples. By examining these case studies, we can see how collective emotion, energy transfer, and micro-signals combine to produce the movements we observe on charts.

The 1987 Stock Market Crash

Known as "Black Monday," October 19, 1987, saw global markets drop precipitously, with the Dow Jones Industrial Average falling over 22% in a single day.

Emotional Dynamics: Fear dominated. Program trading and margin calls amplified anxiety, creating a rapid withdrawal of energy from the market.

Energy Transfer: Selling pressure cascaded as each participant reacted to both prices and the perceived panic of others a massive discharge of emotional energy through the system.

Micro-Signals: Leading up to the crash, subtle signs were visible: spikes in volatility, unusual bid-ask spreads, and small accelerations in selling across multiple asset classes. Traders who recognized these micro-signals could sense the mounting tension before the collapse became obvious.

The Dot-Com Bubble (1999–2000)

The late 1990s were marked by extraordinary optimism in technology stocks, inflating valuations far beyond fundamentals.

Emotional Organism: Collective greed and euphoria created persistent energy inflows into tech equities. Sentiment feedback loops reinforced buying behavior, amplifying trends beyond rational expectation.

Micro-Signals: Early indicators included minor pauses and retracements in individual stock price movements, divergence between volume and price action, and oscillating sentiment in analyst reports. These small signals were harbingers of the instability that would eventually release as a massive correction.

The 2008 Global Financial Crisis

Triggered by the collapse of the U.S. housing market, the 2008 crisis illustrates the interplay of fear, systemic interconnectivity, and feedback loops.

Collective Nervous System: Banks, institutions, and investors were tightly interlinked. Stress in mortgage-backed securities propagated rapidly, transmitting panic throughout global markets.

Energy Dynamics: Withdrawals of capital, margin calls, and sudden risk aversion acted as energy sinks, compressing the market and increasing volatility.

Micro-Signals: Early micro-signals included unusual credit spreads, incremental declines in housing-related equities, and spikes in implied volatility. Observers of these small cues could detect the emergent systemic stress before the full collapse.

Recent Example: 2020 COVID-19 Market Shock

The pandemic-induced sell-off in March 2020 exemplifies the rapid transmission of fear in a hyper-connected, global market.

Emotional Organism: Anxiety about economic disruption triggered unprecedented synchronized selling. Algorithms and human participants reinforced each other, amplifying the pulse of fear.

Energy Transfer: Massive energy outflows occurred across equities, commodities, and derivatives, illustrating how emotional energy can propagate almost instantaneously through the global nervous system.

Micro-Signals: Subtle indicators appeared in increased volatility, erratic intraday swings, and correlated movements across multiple asset classes. Traders who could perceive these micro-signals had an early window into the upcoming large-scale energy release.

Lessons for Traders

From these examples, several key insights emerge:

1. **Emotion Drives Movement:** Fear, greed, and uncertainty dominate market behavior, often more than fundamentals.

2. **Energy Cascades:** Small inputs can trigger massive responses through feedback loops and collective nervous systems.

3. **Micro-Signals Matter:** Subtle, early indicators often precede major trends, corrections, or crashes.

4. **Observation Over Prediction:** Perceiving the market's emotional and energetic state provides more actionable insight than attempting to forecast precise price levels.

Synthesis

These case studies reinforce the concept of the market as a **living, resonant organism**. Historical and recent movements reveal patterns of energy flow, collective cognition, and micro-signals that repeat across time and assets. By learning to sense these dynamics, traders gain an edge not in certainty, but in **alignment with the market's pulse**, navigating its rhythm with awareness and adaptability.

"History does not merely repeat; it resonates. Learn to hear the echoes of past pulses in the present market."

Chapter 2

Waves of Sentiment

Markets, like oceans, are never still. Beneath the surface of price charts lies a continuous ebb and flow the **waves of collective emotion** that surge, collide, and recede with the rhythm of human psychology. Every tick, candle, and trend is shaped not only by fundamental forces but by the **dynamic interplay of fear, greed, hope, and despair** among participants. These emotional waves are the hidden currents that guide price movement, often more powerfully than logic or analysis alone.

In this chapter, we explore how sentiment moves through markets as measurable energy, creating oscillations that manifest as trends, reversals, and volatility. We will map the frequencies of emotion, examine the amplitude of their impact, and uncover the subtle early signals that hint at the direction and strength of upcoming waves.

By understanding the **architecture of sentiment**, traders can begin to perceive the market's underlying energy, anticipating movements with awareness rather than reacting to them blindly. This chapter bridges the conceptual with the practical, providing a framework for observing, measuring, and aligning with the emotional currents that shape every market decision.

2.1 Fear, Greed, Hope, and Despair

Markets are not just driven by fundamentals or data; they are the **manifestation of collective human emotion**. Every price move, trend, and reversal carries the imprint of the emotions that flow through participants from fleeting micro-decisions to the dominant moods of entire market segments. Among these emotions, four primary currents shape the pulse of markets: **fear, greed, hope, and despair**. Understanding their dynamics is essential for reading the hidden energy beneath price action.

Fear: The Constricting Force

Fear is the contraction of market energy. It triggers **withdrawal, hesitation, and reactive selling**, reducing liquidity and amplifying volatility.

Behavioral Manifestations:

- Rapid liquidation of positions during small losses.
- Tight stop losses and avoidance of new entries.
- Increased sensitivity to news or rumors.

Market Signatures:

- Sharp price declines with accelerating volume.
- Intraday spikes in volatility.
- Rejection of new highs or resistance levels.

Trading Implications: Recognizing fear micro-signals allows traders to anticipate oversold conditions, potential rebounds, or periods of market compression. Traders aligned with energy flow may choose to observe, wait, or selectively position themselves ahead of a relief rally.

Greed: The Expanding Force

Greed is the expansion of energy, driving **momentum, trend amplification, and exuberant participation**. It is often contagious, spreading through both retail and institutional participants.

Behavioral Manifestations:

- Aggressive buying and leverage accumulation.
- Chasing rallies or entering positions near peaks.
- Overconfidence in trend continuation.

Market Signatures:

- Rapid upward price movement with strong volume.
- Breakouts extending beyond prior resistance levels.
- High valuation or deviation from fundamentals.

Trading Implications: Detecting peaks of greed can indicate areas of potential exhaustion. Traders can use these signals to manage risk, reduce exposure, or anticipate trend reversals.

Hope: The Sustaining Current

Hope is subtler but no less powerful. It underpins **gradual recovery, tentative buying, and endurance in the face of uncertainty**. Hope maintains the market's energy during corrections and consolidations, acting as a stabilizing force.

Behavioral Manifestations:

- Cautious accumulation of positions.
- Holding through volatility with measured risk.
- Optimistic response to small positive news.

Market Signatures:

- Gradual upward drift in price during consolidations.
- Modest volume spikes as participants re-enter carefully.
- Sideways oscillations with positive bias.

Trading Implications: Hope-driven behavior signals **accumulation phases**, providing clues for trend continuation or potential breakout points. Observing these currents allows traders to align with emergent energy.

Despair: The Release and Reset

Despair occurs when optimism collapses and **emotional energy is drained from the market**. It often follows extended losses, shocks, or failures of confidence, triggering **capitulation and extreme risk aversion**.

Behavioral Manifestations:

- Panic selling and mass exit from positions.
- Abandonment of strategies and withdrawal from markets.
- Emotional decision-making dominating rational assessment.

Market Signatures:

- Sharp, rapid declines often exceeding fundamental justification.
- Liquidity shortages and large bid-ask spreads.
- High intraday volatility with extreme price swings.

Trading Implications: Despair often precedes market bottoms. Traders who can sense these micro-signals may identify **contrarian opportunities**, entering at points where the majority has exhausted emotional energy.

Oscillation and Interplay

These four emotional currents do not exist in isolation. Markets oscillate between them:

- Fear can escalate into despair if selling pressure dominates.
- Greed often peaks before hope fades, eventually triggering fear.
- Hope mitigates despair, enabling gradual recovery and trend continuation.

By understanding the **frequency, amplitude, and interaction** of these emotions, traders can perceive the market's energetic rhythm, anticipate turning points, and make decisions **in resonance with collective sentiment** rather than in opposition to it.

Conclusion

Fear, greed, hope, and despair form the **emotional lattice of markets**, influencing every price movement, trend, and correction. Mastering market awareness requires **attunement to these currents**, recognizing both subtle micro-signals and dominant waves, and aligning action with the natural oscillation of human emotion in the market.

"To understand the market is to understand the heartbeat of humanity itself its hopes, fears, desires, and doubts, all flowing together in a living rhythm."

2.2 Emotional Frequency Mapping

Just as sound waves carry energy at different frequencies, market emotions oscillate at **distinct frequencies** that influence price behavior. **Emotional frequency mapping** is the process of observing, measuring, and visualizing these oscillations to understand the underlying market dynamics.

Defining Emotional Frequencies

Every collective emotion fear, greed, hope, despair can be thought of as a **vibrational state of the market's energy**.

- **High-frequency emotions** appear rapidly, often in intraday trading or micro-movements. Examples include sudden bursts of fear or spikes of greed.

- **Low-frequency emotions** unfold over longer periods, shaping daily, weekly, or monthly trends. Examples include sustained hope during accumulation or extended despair during market crashes.

Mapping these frequencies allows traders to **discern the tempo of sentiment**, distinguishing transient noise from sustained energy that drives significant trends.

Amplitude and Energy Levels

Frequency alone is insufficient. The **amplitude of emotional oscillation** reflects the intensity of collective sentiment:

- **High amplitude:** Intense fear or euphoric greed, often corresponding to volatility spikes or rapid price movements.
- **Low amplitude:** Mild hope or subdued concern, seen in quiet consolidation periods or minor corrections.

By observing both **frequency and amplitude**, traders gain a **two-dimensional understanding** of market energy: how quickly sentiment changes, and how forcefully it manifests.

Visualization Techniques

Emotional frequency can be represented through conceptual or quantitative visualizations:

- **Oscillation charts:** Plot sentiment intensity over time, highlighting peaks of fear, greed, hope, or despair.
- **Volume-weighted sentiment curves:** Overlay emotional estimates with trade volume to reflect the magnitude of participant engagement.
- **Cross-asset frequency correlation:** Compare oscillations across equities, commodities, or indices to detect synchronous emotional shifts.

These tools provide a **mental map of market rhythm**, enabling the trader to align strategy with the dominant currents rather than reacting blindly to price.

Identifying Resonance and Dissonance

Markets are most predictable when the **emotional frequency aligns across participants** a state of resonance.

- **Resonance:** Collective sentiment moves in phase, producing strong trends and coherent energy flow.

- **Dissonance:** Sentiment oscillates out of phase, with conflicting micro-signals, indecision, and choppy price action.

Mapping emotional frequency allows traders to **anticipate periods of coherence**, where trends can be trusted, versus periods of dissonance, where caution is warranted.

Practical Application for Traders

1. **Observe multi-timeframe sentiment:** Track short-term micro-frequencies alongside long-term emotional cycles. 2. **Measure amplitude:** Estimate the intensity of current market emotion through volatility, volume, and micro-signal analysis. 3. **Detect emerging resonance:** Identify areas where multiple assets or sectors show aligned emotional frequency, signaling stronger trend potential. 4. **Calibrate decision-making:** Use frequency mapping to avoid overreacting to isolated spikes, and to enter trades in alignment with prevailing market energy. 5. **Journal and refine:** Record observations of emotional frequency, market outcomes, and personal decision alignment to build perceptual sensitivity over time.

Conclusion

Emotional frequency mapping transforms abstract sentiment into **actionable insight**. By perceiving both the tempo and intensity of market emotions, traders gain a **conceptual compass**, enabling decisions that flow with the collective pulse rather than against it. In essence, understanding emotional frequency is learning to "hear" the market's hidden rhythm and align with it consciously.

"Markets do not move randomly; they oscillate to the emotional frequencies of the collective mind. Learn to tune your perception to their pulse."

2.3 Amplitude and Volatility

In the study of market sentiment, **amplitude** refers to the intensity of collective emotion, while **volatility** represents the observable manifestation of that emotional energy in price movements. Understanding the relationship between emotional amplitude and market volatility allows traders to interpret not just the direction of price moves, but the **strength and urgency behind them**.

Defining Amplitude in Market Sentiment

Amplitude measures the **magnitude of emotional energy** within the market at a given moment:

- **High amplitude:** Extreme fear, greed, or hope, often corresponding to frenzied buying or panic selling.
- **Low amplitude:** Mild concern or optimism, associated with calm, consolidating markets.

Amplitude can be detected through multiple indicators:

- Rapid swings in price over short periods
- Spikes in trading volume or liquidity shifts
- Heightened news sensitivity or social sentiment surges

Volatility as Emotional Manifestation

Volatility is the **physical expression of emotional amplitude** in market behavior. A market's price oscillations reflect the collective intensity of sentiment:

- **High volatility:** Strong emotions dominate; prices fluctuate aggressively, often forming sharp peaks or troughs.
- **Low volatility:** Calm emotional states prevail; prices move steadily with minimal disruption.

By tracking volatility alongside emotional micro-signals, traders can **infer the underlying emotional amplitude**, even when the market seems quiet or orderly.

Amplitude-Volatility Relationship

Emotional amplitude and market volatility are deeply interconnected:

1. **Extreme amplitude generates volatility:** Panic selling or euphoric buying causes sudden, large price swings.
2. **Moderate amplitude produces measured trends:** Balanced sentiment yields smooth price movements.
3. **Low amplitude results in consolidation:** Neutral or indecisive sentiment creates tight ranges with low volume and minimal directional movement.

Recognizing this relationship allows traders to **anticipate market behavior** before price moves fully materialize.

Amplitude Across Timeframes

Emotional amplitude can vary across **short-term and long-term timeframes:**

- **Intraday amplitude:** Rapid fear or greed pulses appear in high-frequency trading or algorithmic spikes.
- **Intermediate amplitude:** Multi-day trends reflect sustained emotional energy in retail and institutional participation.
- **Long-term amplitude:** Extended cycles of hope or despair can drive multi-week or multi-month trends.

Traders who observe amplitude across timeframes gain a **multi-dimensional understanding** of market energy and trend potential.

Practical Application

1. **Identify amplitude spikes:** Look for sudden surges in volume, price movement, or social sentiment indicators. 2. **Adjust risk accordingly:** High-amplitude environments often require smaller position sizes or disciplined stops to manage energy-induced volatility. 3. **Align entries with amplitude:** Enter trades when amplitude indicates a clear directional bias rather than when sentiment is chaotic or conflicting. 4. **Observe decay:** After peak amplitude events, markets often revert to lower-volatility states, signaling potential consolidation or reversal.

Conclusion

Amplitude and volatility are the **twin expressions of market energy** the first invisible, psychological and emotional, the second visible, mechanical, and measurable. By understanding this connection, traders move beyond surface-level chart analysis to **perceive the intensity behind price action**, allowing for alignment with the market's emotional rhythm rather than mere reaction to its movements.

"Price moves are only the surface. The depth is in the intensity of the emotion that drives them."

2.4 Subtle Early Signals of Market Movement

While markets often move in dramatic waves of fear, greed, hope, or despair, these large swings are usually preceded by **subtle micro-signals**. These early cues, often imperceptible to most participants, provide traders with a **foresight advantage**, allowing them to align with the underlying flow before major trends become obvious.

What Are Early Signals?

Early signals are the **initial tremors of collective sentiment**, small behavioral or quantitative changes that hint at larger market moves:

- Minor price deviations or unusual micro-candlestick patterns
- Sudden changes in trading volume within low-activity periods
- Shifts in bid-ask spreads or order book imbalances
- Emerging trends in social sentiment or news flow

These signals are often subtle and require **attuned perception**, careful observation, and contextual interpretation.

Behavioral Micro-Signals

Emotional micro-signals manifest through trader behavior before major moves:

- **Accumulation or distribution in small increments:** Informed participants quietly buy or sell, creating gentle pressure on prices.
- **Hesitation or indecision:** Minor oscillations, repeated retests of support/resistance, or unusual cancellation of orders indicate uncertainty that often precedes sharp movements.
- **Patterned reaction to news:** Subtle overreactions or underreactions to minor events signal emotional bias building in the market.

Recognizing these behaviors provides insight into **sentiment alignment and the potential direction of the next wave**.

Quantitative Micro-Signals

In addition to behavioral cues, small-scale quantitative changes can act as early warning signs:

- **Micro-volatility shifts:** Slight upticks in intraday volatility may precede larger swings.
- **Volume anomalies:** Small but consistent deviations from average volume highlight early participation shifts.
- **Correlation changes:** Divergence or convergence among related assets can indicate emerging sentiment shifts across sectors or markets.

These subtle indicators allow traders to **detect the emotional energy building beneath the surface**, long before the full wave becomes visible in price charts.

Timing and Context

Early signals are only meaningful when interpreted within **context**:

- Market phase (accumulation, trending, consolidation)
- Broader macro or sectoral news
- Timeframe alignment across micro and macro oscillations

A micro-signal in isolation may be noise, but **when multiple cues converge**, the probability of a meaningful move increases significantly.

Practical Application

1. **Observe micro-price patterns:** Look for repeated subtle movements that deviate from average ranges. 2. **Track volume anomalies:** Small surges in volume can precede trend acceleration. 3. **Monitor sentiment feeds:** Social and news sentiment can provide leading clues about market emotion. 4. **Cross-check across assets:** Early signals often appear in related markets before propagating broadly. 5. **Calibrate risk:** Use these early insights to position cautiously, with an awareness that signals may still evolve.

Conclusion

Subtle early signals are the **footholds of foresight**. They reveal the **initial emotional energy** before it erupts into visible price movement. Traders who attune themselves to these micro-cues gain the ability to **anticipate trends, act in alignment with emerging sentiment, and navigate the market with greater awareness and precision**.

"The market whispers before it roars. Those who listen closely catch the current before it becomes a wave."

Chapter 3

Resonance Loops

Markets are not static entities; they are **living, dynamic systems**, where every action reverberates through the collective network of participants. A single trade, a subtle shift in sentiment, or even a rumor can trigger a cascade of reactions that amplify far beyond the initial input. These reverberations form what we call **resonance loops** cycles of feedback between trader behavior and market response that create emergent patterns, trends, and sometimes unexpected outcomes.

In this chapter, we explore how individual and collective actions **interact with market energy**, creating self-reinforcing cycles or destructive feedback. We will examine how small inputs can lead to outsized effects, why some loops amplify momentum while others dissipate, and how understanding these loops allows traders to **align their decisions with the market's natural rhythm** rather than fight against it.

Through the lens of resonance loops, markets become more than charts or indicators they reveal themselves as **responsive systems**, where awareness, timing, and emotional calibration determine not only survival but mastery. The following sections break down the mechanics of these loops and provide frameworks for recognizing, anticipating, and leveraging them in trading practice.

3.1 Feedback Between Trader Decisions and Market Reaction

Markets are inherently interactive systems where **every trader's decision sends ripples through the collective consciousness**. This interplay between individual action and market response forms the foundation of **feedback loops**, shaping trends, amplifying volatility, and influencing the behavior of other participants. Understanding this feedback is critical for perceiving markets not just as price charts, but as **dynamic, responsive organisms**.

The Mechanism of Feedback

A feedback loop occurs when a trader's action generates a **market reaction**, which in turn influences subsequent decisions:

- **Positive (reinforcing) feedback:** A small purchase triggers rising prices, encouraging more buying and creating a momentum-driven trend.
- **Negative (balancing) feedback:** A sale causes prices to fall, prompting caution or buying at perceived lows, which stabilizes the market.

These loops can operate at **multiple scales** from micro-level intraday trades to macro-level trend cycles and are **amplified by collective behavior**.

Trader Psychology in Feedback Loops

Trader perception plays a crucial role in shaping feedback:

- **Expectation amplification:** Belief that prices will rise or fall causes actions that partially fulfill those expectations, creating self-fulfilling dynamics.
- **Herding behavior:** Observing others' actions reinforces individual decisions, often accelerating momentum.
- **Overreaction and underreaction:** Emotional intensity can magnify or suppress feedback effects, affecting trend strength and volatility.

By observing **how decisions propagate and interact**, traders can anticipate potential accelerations or slowdowns in market movement.

Micro vs Macro Feedback

- **Micro-feedback loops:** Rapid interactions between a few participants or algorithmic trades, often visible in short-term volatility.
- **Macro-feedback loops:** Larger-scale cycles involving sentiment, media influence, and institutional behavior, shaping multi-day or multi-week trends.

Both scales operate simultaneously, creating a **nested hierarchy of resonance**, where small micro-decisions can cascade into significant macro consequences.

Practical Implications for Traders

1. **Observe your influence:** Recognize that even small actions may contribute to broader market behavior. 2. **Read market responses:** Notice how your trades and external events trigger reactions; these are signals of emerging loops. 3. **Align with reinforcing cycles:** Enter positions when feedback loops support your directional bias, amplifying momentum. 4. **Avoid destructive loops:** Refrain from fighting strong reinforcing sentiment without clear evidence; misalignment can increase risk. 5. **Calibrate decision timing:** Subtle micro-signals in feedback loops often precede larger moves, providing opportunities for early, low-risk positioning.

Conclusion

Feedback loops reveal the **co-creative nature of markets** individual actions shape collective outcomes, which in turn influence the next set of actions. By understanding this cycle, traders gain **situational awareness** and the ability to align with the natural resonance of market energy, rather than reacting blindly to price.

"In every market ripple, there is a reflection of action observe it, and you begin to see the wave before it arrives."

3.2 Small Inputs Leading to Large Amplifications

Markets are highly **nonlinear systems**, meaning that tiny actions or shifts in sentiment can produce disproportionately large effects. This phenomenon where **small inputs trigger amplified market reactions** is a core principle of resonance loops and underpins the dynamics of volatility, trend acceleration, and sudden reversals.

The Butterfly Effect in Markets

Borrowing from chaos theory, markets exhibit a "**butterfly effect**":

- A single trade, rumor, or sentiment shift can set off a chain reaction, influencing other participants.
- Each subsequent reaction can further amplify the original input, creating a **cumulative impact far exceeding the initial action**.
- The effect is magnified in tightly coupled systems where traders, algorithms, and media interact in real-time.

This nonlinearity explains why **minor news events or micro-level decisions** can sometimes generate outsized market moves.

Mechanics of Amplification

Amplification occurs through **feedback and connectivity**:

- **Positive reinforcement:** Early buyers or sellers trigger price changes that attract more participants.
- **Network effects:** Traders observe the behavior of others, causing cascading responses across markets or sectors.
- **Psychological contagion:** Emotions like fear or greed propagate quickly, converting small sentiment shifts into major market energy.

Even seemingly insignificant inputs like a marginal increase in buy orders or a subtle shift in sentiment on social media can **cascade through these channels**.

Historical and Recent Examples

- **Flash crashes:** Minor imbalances or algorithmic errors have led to sudden, massive price swings in milliseconds.
- **Momentum rallies:** Early accumulation by informed traders can spark waves of buying that grow exponentially as more participants join.
- **Sentiment-driven moves:** Small news items or tweets can ignite panic or euphoria, amplifying price movement beyond fundamental justification.

These examples illustrate the **power of small inputs in shaping large-scale market behavior**.

Recognizing Amplification Potential

Traders can develop awareness of conditions conducive to amplification:

- **High connectivity:** When markets are tightly coupled across assets, sectors, or platforms.
- **Elevated emotional energy:** Fear, greed, or hope is already high, making participants more sensitive to inputs.
- **Low liquidity or thin order books:** Small trades have disproportionate price impact.

Recognizing these conditions allows traders to **anticipate where minor signals may cascade**, and position accordingly.

Practical Applications for Traders

1. **Observe micro-movements:** Early, subtle price or volume changes often precede amplified trends. 2. **Assess context:** Identify whether emotional energy and market connectivity are high, which increases amplification potential. 3. **Position with caution:** Enter trades aligned with emergent momentum, but manage risk, as amplified moves can reverse quickly. 4. **Leverage observation over action:** Sometimes the greatest advantage is noticing the initial tremors without immediately participating, allowing clearer decision-making as trends unfold.

Conclusion

Small inputs can wield extraordinary influence in markets due to **feedback loops, psychological contagion, and networked interactions**. Mastery lies in **detecting these micro-signals early, understanding the conditions for amplification, and aligning actions with the market's emergent energy**, rather than reacting to visible outcomes alone.

"The quietest whisper can stir a wave; the attuned observer moves with it, not against it."

3.3 Constructive vs. Destructive Loops

Not all resonance loops influence markets positively. Some **reinforce alignment and momentum**, while others **amplify instability and chaos**. Understanding the distinction between **constructive and destructive loops** is essential for traders seeking to navigate the market's emotional and energetic landscape effectively.

Defining Constructive Loops

A constructive loop occurs when **feedback between trader actions and market response enhances clarity, coherence, and trend stability**:

- Small, aligned inputs amplify existing momentum without creating disorder.
- Market participants act in resonance, reinforcing confidence in directional moves.
- Trends become predictable, allowing informed traders to align with the collective rhythm.

Example: During a steady uptrend, incremental buying by early informed traders triggers rising prices. Observing this trend, other participants add positions, reinforcing momentum while volatility remains moderate. The loop sustains growth without triggering panic or abrupt reversals.

Defining Destructive Loops

A destructive loop arises when **feedback amplifies misalignment, fear, or emotional overreaction**, destabilizing the market:

- Conflicting inputs collide, producing erratic price behavior.
- Amplified fear or greed leads to overshooting, rapid reversals, or flash crashes.
- Emotional contagion overrides rational assessment, creating temporary chaos.

Example: A rumor triggers initial selling in a thinly traded market. Fear spreads, causing panic selling, further price drops, margin calls, and abrupt volatility spikes. The destructive loop magnifies instability far beyond the initial trigger.

Key Factors Determining Loop Type

Several factors influence whether a loop is constructive or destructive:

- **Alignment of sentiment:** Loops are constructive when participants share a coherent understanding or bias; destructive when sentiment is fragmented.
- **Market liquidity:** Ample liquidity absorbs shocks, supporting constructive loops; thin markets are prone to destructive amplification.
- **Feedback velocity:** Rapid, uncontrolled feedback can escalate into destructive loops; measured, deliberate responses favor constructive resonance.
- **External stressors:** Economic shocks, unexpected news, or geopolitical events can transform otherwise constructive loops into destructive ones.

Recognizing Loops in Practice

- Monitor **volatility relative to trend:** Constructive loops maintain moderate volatility; destructive loops show spikes or erratic swings.
- Track **participation coherence:** Are traders moving in alignment with the trend, or acting out of fear and uncertainty?

- Observe **feedback timing:** Constructive loops evolve gradually, allowing anticipation; destructive loops escalate rapidly, often catching participants off-guard.

Practical Trading Insights

1. **Align with constructive loops:** Identify periods where collective sentiment, trend, and momentum reinforce one another. Positioning during these loops increases the probability of sustained success. 2. **Avoid destructive loops:** Recognize early signs of chaos, such as rapid reversals, fragmented participation, and extreme emotional swings. Minimize exposure or use risk-control strategies. 3. **Use loops as learning tools:** Observe how loops form, escalate, and resolve. This enhances awareness of market psychology and improves decision-making calibration. 4. **Maintain emotional discipline:** Constructive loops reward alignment and patience; destructive loops punish impulsive, emotionally reactive behavior.

Conclusion

Understanding **constructive and destructive loops** transforms the trader's perspective from reactive to **systemic awareness**. Markets are not merely price charts; they are dynamic systems where energy, emotion, and decision-making interact continuously. By recognizing the type of loop in play, traders can **align with market resonance, mitigate risk, and harness the flow of collective behavior** for better timing, positioning, and insight.

"Some loops lift the tide, others churn the storm. Mastery is in seeing the difference and navigating with awareness."

Chapter 4

Flow vs. Noise

Markets are saturated with information, opinions, and signals, yet only a fraction of this input reflects **true underlying market dynamics**. The rest is **noise** random fluctuations, misleading patterns, or emotionally charged reactions that obscure genuine opportunities. Learning to **distinguish flow from noise** is a critical skill for traders seeking alignment with the market's natural rhythm.

In this chapter, we explore how traders can **synchronize their mind with market energy**, filter out distractions, and recognize authentic signals that emerge from collective behavior. We will examine techniques for detecting true resonance, avoiding false alignment, and calibrating perception to the subtle movements of emotional and cognitive energy within markets.

By understanding flow versus noise, traders gain the ability to act **with intention rather than reaction**, navigating markets with clarity, patience, and strategic precision. The following sections break down the mechanics of alignment, signal recognition, and false resonance, offering both conceptual frameworks and practical exercises for applied mastery.

4.1 Aligning Mind with Market Rhythm

Trading successfully is not only about analyzing charts or executing strategies it is about **tuning the mind to the market's intrinsic energy and flow**. Markets are dynamic systems, driven by the collective emotions, beliefs, and actions of all participants. When a trader's mind aligns with this rhythm, decisions become **intuitive, precise, and responsive**, reducing noise-driven errors and enhancing awareness of emergent patterns.

The Nature of Market Rhythm

Market rhythm emerges from the **cyclical interplay of sentiment and action**:

- **Emotional waves:** Fear, greed, hope, and indecision propagate through the trader network, creating identifiable pulses in market behavior.
- **Volatility cycles:** Rapid bursts of activity alternate with calmer consolidations, reflecting the natural ebb and flow of energy in the system.
- **Trend formation:** Sustained directional movement occurs when the collective resonance of market participants is coherent.

By perceiving these cycles, traders gain insight into **when to act, when to wait, and when to observe**, moving in sync with the system rather than against it.

Techniques for Mind-Market Synchronization

Achieving alignment requires deliberate practice and awareness:

1. **Mindful Observation:** Observe price, volume, and sentiment objectively. Avoid instant judgment or reaction; note patterns, oscillations, and emerging signals.
2. **Emotional Calibration:** Use breathing exercises, meditation, or brief pauses to stabilize your internal state. Emotional coherence enhances the ability to detect subtle market cues.
3. **Pattern Recognition Across Scales:** Track repetitive micro oscillations and macro-cycles. Recognize the fractal nature of market flow micro-movements often reflect larger patterns.
4. **Tempo Matching:** Adjust your trading pace to match market energy. Avoid forcing trades during low-amplitude or chaotic phases; act when the system's rhythm is coherent.

Signs of Alignment vs. Disconnection

Indicators of alignment:

- Smooth, consistent trends with moderate volatility
- Clear cause-effect relationships between market events and price action
- Calm, focused, and adaptive mental state

Indicators of disconnection:

- Erratic price swings with unpredictable reactions
- Frequent surprise, frustration, or impulsive decision-making
- Emotional overreaction or compulsive trading behavior

Practical Applications for Traders

- **Pre-session alignment:** Spend a few minutes centering attention, observing market pre-open patterns, and assessing sentiment energy.
- **Active observation:** Continuously track micro-fluctuations, volume spikes, and sentiment changes to identify alignment windows.
- **Timing entries and exits:** Initiate trades when the market is in a coherent state; avoid forcing trades during high-disorder phases.
- **Reflective journaling:** After sessions, record observations about alignment, market rhythm, and decision coherence to improve future synchronization.

Conclusion

Aligning the mind with market rhythm transforms trading from **reactive behavior into intentional participation**. It is not about predicting every move but about **perceiving the underlying flow of collective energy** and acting in resonance with it. Traders who achieve this alignment experience clarity, patience, and strategic insight, turning each decision into a conscious dialogue with the market.

> *"The market has a pulse; mastery is in feeling it, moving with it, and not against it."*

4.2 Recognizing True Signals Amidst Noise

In every market, there exists an overwhelming amount of data, commentary, and price movement. Much of it is **noise** random fluctuations, emotionally-driven reactions, or irrelevant information. The challenge for traders is to **filter out this noise and identify true signals** that reflect the underlying rhythm and energy of the market.

Understanding Noise vs. Signal

- **Noise:** Random price movements, conflicting indicators, impulsive reactions, and transient market chatter. Noise can obscure meaningful patterns and trigger premature or reactive decisions.
- **Signal:** Patterns, trends, or micro-behaviors that reliably indicate the direction, intensity, or emotional momentum of the market. Signals are often subtle and require **attuned observation and context** to recognize.

Sources of Noise

Noise arises from multiple factors:

- **Short-term volatility:** Small orders or algorithmic trades can create temporary fluctuations that do not reflect genuine sentiment.
- **Media and social amplification:** Headlines, tweets, and rumors can provoke emotional reactions, producing misleading price swings.
- **Cognitive bias:** Traders may perceive patterns where none exist, projecting narratives onto random events.

Techniques for Identifying True Signals

1. **Contextual Analysis:** - Compare current price action with historical patterns, emotional cycles, and macro conditions. - Evaluate whether observed movements align with the market's underlying rhythm.

2. **Multi-Timeframe Observation:** - Signals often reveal themselves more clearly when viewed across different timeframes. - Micro-fluctuations should be assessed within the context of larger trends to separate noise from meaningful movements.

3. **Emotional Energy Mapping:** - Track collective sentiment indicators such as fear/greed indices, volume surges, or social sentiment. - Genuine signals often correspond with coherent shifts in emotional energy rather than isolated spikes.

4. **Confirmation Across Dimensions:** - Cross-check potential signals across correlated assets, volume patterns, and volatility measures. - True signals exhibit resonance across multiple dimensions; noise tends to remain isolated.

Recognizing Signal Patterns

- **Consistent directional moves:** Gradual accumulation or distribution with coherent momentum.
- **Aligned sentiment shifts:** Collective behavior that reinforces the observed trend.
- **Micro-oscillation coherence:** Small fluctuations that echo broader market cycles, indicating emerging energy alignment.

Practical Application

- **Observation over reaction:** Wait for confirmation before acting; avoid reacting to isolated spikes or rumors. - **Journaling:** Record suspected signals, the context, and subsequent outcomes to refine detection skills. - **Risk calibration:** Even when signals are identified, align position size and timing with confidence in the signal and market energy. - **Iterative refinement:** Over time, develop a personal framework for distinguishing noise from meaningful patterns based on experience, observation, and reflection.

Conclusion

Markets are a continuous interplay of noise and signal. Mastery lies in **training perception to detect the subtle currents beneath superficial movements**, enabling traders to act **with clarity, precision, and resonance**. By recognizing true signals amidst noise, traders not only improve execution but also cultivate a **deeper intuitive understanding of market energy**.

"Amid the clamor of the market, it is the quiet, coherent signal that guides the attuned observer."

4.3 Avoiding False Resonance

In trading, not every alignment or pattern that appears coherent is genuine. Sometimes the mind perceives a resonance that **does not exist in the market's collective energy**. This is what we call **false resonance** an apparent signal that lures traders into premature or misguided action. Recognizing and avoiding false resonance is essential for maintaining clarity, discipline, and long-term success.

What Is False Resonance?

False resonance occurs when:

- Patterns appear aligned but are driven by **random fluctuations or transient noise**.
- Trader perception is influenced by **cognitive biases**, projecting expectations onto the market.
- Emotional states greed, fear, or hope create the illusion of coherence where none exists.

Unlike true resonance, false resonance often leads to **erratic entries, amplified losses, and emotional frustration**.

Common Sources of False Resonance

- **Short-lived trends:** Rapid spikes or dips that reverse quickly, creating a misleading sense of momentum.
- **Confirmation bias:** Seeing patterns that confirm pre-existing beliefs rather than objective observation.
- **Over-reliance on indicators:** Technical or sentiment indicators can generate apparent alignment that is not reflected in actual market behavior.
- **Herd mimicry:** Following collective behavior without verifying underlying energy can create a false sense of resonance.

Techniques to Avoid False Resonance

1. **Multiple Confirmations:** - Verify potential resonance across different dimensions: price action, volume, correlated assets, and emotional sentiment. - True resonance shows coherence across several indicators; false resonance is inconsistent.

2. **Temporal Consistency:** - Observe whether alignment sustains over multiple timeframes. - True resonance persists and evolves; false resonance dissipates quickly.

3. **Emotional Awareness:** - Identify whether perception is influenced by emotional states such as anxiety, excitement, or attachment to a preconceived outcome. - Practice mindfulness and reflective pauses before acting.

4. **Risk-Aware Testing:** - Enter small, measured positions to validate perceived resonance. - Observe outcomes and adjust perception before committing significant capital.

Practical Strategies

- Maintain a **calibrated mental state**: Use journaling and reflection to separate expectation from observation.
- **Patience over impulsivity**: Wait for confirmation, avoiding the temptation to act on surface-level patterns.
- **Observe divergence**: If price action, volume, and sentiment do not align coherently, treat it as noise.
- **Iterative learning**: Record false resonance instances to refine recognition skills and improve future decision-making.

Conclusion

False resonance is a natural challenge for any trader attuned to market rhythms. The key is not to eliminate perception but to **develop the discernment to differentiate true alignment from illusion**. By applying awareness, multi-dimensional validation, and disciplined action, traders can minimize costly missteps, strengthen mental calibration, and consistently act in harmony with the market's authentic flow.

"The market whispers its truths; the untrained mind often hears only echoes of its own expectation."

Chapter 5

Market Harmonics

Markets are not random; they move in **rhythms, cycles, and oscillations** that emerge from the collective behavior of traders and the flow of emotional energy. Understanding these **market harmonics** the micro-oscillations of short-term sentiment and the macro-cycles of long-term trends allows traders to anticipate turning points, optimize timing, and align decisions with the natural cadence of the system.

In this chapter, we explore the concept of market harmonics as a **bridge between observation and action**. We examine how subtle fluctuations aggregate into larger patterns, how emotional waves rise and fall, and how recognition of these rhythms can transform trading from reactive behavior into **flow-aligned execution**.

Through a combination of conceptual frameworks, practical techniques, and illustrative examples, this chapter provides tools to sense and leverage the underlying oscillatory structure of markets. By mastering market harmonics, traders gain the ability to **navigate both micro and macro dynamics**, detect emerging opportunities early, and make decisions that resonate with the system rather than against it.

5.1 Micro-Oscillations and Macro-Cycles

Markets are composed of layers of oscillatory behavior, from **minute-to-minute fluctuations** to **multi-year trend cycles**. Understanding the relationship between these micro-oscillations and macro-cycles is essential for sensing the rhythm of the market, anticipating turning points, and making decisions that align with the collective flow of trader behavior.

Defining Micro-Oscillations

- Micro-oscillations are **short-term, small amplitude movements** in price and sentiment.

- They reflect the **immediate emotional responses** of market participants reactions to news, rumors, or intraday order flow.
- While subtle, micro-oscillations often contain **early indicators of larger trends**, acting as a high-resolution signal of underlying energy shifts.

Understanding Macro-Cycles

- Macro-cycles are **longer-term patterns**, often spanning weeks, months, or years.
- They emerge from **collective behavior, structural economic shifts, and recurring emotional patterns** in markets.
- Macro-cycles provide context to micro-movements, helping traders distinguish between transient noise and sustained trends.

The Interplay Between Micro and Macro

- Micro-oscillations are the **building blocks** of macro-cycles. Small, repeated patterns of accumulation or distribution can aggregate into significant long-term trends.
- Macro-cycles influence the amplitude and frequency of micro-oscillations. For example, during a strong bullish macro-cycle, minor dips are often absorbed quickly, whereas in a bearish macro-cycle, small rallies may fail to sustain.
- Recognizing this **nested structure** allows traders to interpret short-term movements within a broader context, reducing reaction to false signals.

Practical Observations for Traders

1. **Multi-timeframe analysis:** Observe price and sentiment across different timeframes to see how micro-fluctuations align with or diverge from macro-trends.
2. **Amplitude and frequency monitoring:** Track the size and speed of micro-oscillations; larger, coherent oscillations often precede major trend changes.
3. **Contextual decision-making:** Avoid overreacting to micro-oscillations when they are consistent with the overarching macro-cycle; conversely, pay attention when short-term signals contradict long-term trends.
4. **Emotional calibration:** Use micro-oscillation observations to gauge collective sentiment shifts without letting momentary fluctuations trigger impulsive trades.

Examples of Nested Oscillations

- During the 2008 financial crisis, micro-oscillations in the credit and equity markets revealed early signs of panic weeks before macro-cycles confirmed a systemic downturn.
- In recent crypto markets, daily micro-momentum swings often foreshadow larger weekly or monthly cycles, providing observant traders with early alignment opportunities.

Conclusion

Recognizing the **interconnectedness of micro-oscillations and macro-cycles** transforms market observation from a reactive practice into a **resonant, anticipatory skill**. By seeing short-term fluctuations as expressions of long-term cycles, traders can act with precision, enter trades at opportune moments, and maintain clarity even amidst volatility. Mastering this nested rhythm is a crucial step toward trading in **harmony with market energy** rather than against it.

"The small waves reveal the pulse of the ocean; to master the tide, one must read both."

5.2 Timing Emotional Waves

Markets move not only through economic or technical drivers but also through the **ebb and flow of collective emotion**. These emotional waves composed of fear, greed, hope, and uncertainty create rhythms that influence both price and trader behavior. Mastering the timing of these waves allows traders to **align their actions with market energy**, enhancing both precision and resilience.

Understanding Emotional Waves

- Emotional waves are **collective shifts in sentiment** across market participants.
- They manifest as patterns of acceleration and deceleration in price, volatility, and volume.
- The amplitude of a wave reflects the intensity of collective emotion, while its frequency reflects the speed of sentiment oscillation.

Phases of Emotional Waves

Emotional waves generally move through identifiable phases:

1. **Accumulation:** Gradual increase in optimism or pessimism; early-stage sentiment shifts begin to influence trading behavior.

2. **Momentum Build-up:** Growing participation amplifies the wave, creating recognizable trends and stronger directional movement.

3. **Peak Emotion:** Maximum intensity of fear or greed; often coincides with extreme market prices or overextended moves.

4. **Dissipation / Reversal:** Sentiment begins to fade or reverse, signaling potential trend exhaustion or the emergence of a new cycle.

Techniques for Timing Emotional Waves

1. **Observation of Micro-Signals:** - Track subtle changes in volume, volatility, and market chatter. - Early recognition of wave initiation allows positioning before broader participation amplifies movement.

2. **Sentiment Mapping:** - Use tools such as fear/greed indices, order flow sentiment, or social media sentiment analytics. - Map these indicators against price action to identify when waves are strengthening or weakening.

3. **Pattern Recognition:** - Emotional waves often create recurring shapes: spikes, oscillations, and consolidation patterns. - Recognizing these allows traders to anticipate both continuation and reversal points.

4. **Synchronization with Flow:** - Align trades with the rising or falling phase of the emotional wave rather than against it. - Avoid forcing trades during low-coherence periods or when waves are dissipating.

Practical Applications

- **Entry timing:** Initiate positions during early accumulation or momentum build-up phases.

- **Exit timing:** Consider scaling out near peak emotion or at the start of dissipation.

- **Risk modulation:** Adjust position size according to wave amplitude; larger waves can tolerate bigger exposure if aligned correctly.

- **Reflective journaling:** Record wave characteristics, timing decisions, and outcomes to refine future recognition and reaction.

Examples of Emotional Wave Timing

- During the Dot-com bubble, early adopters recognized accumulation and momentum phases, while late participants entered near peak emotion, often at the top.
- In recent cryptocurrency markets, small micro-oscillations often signal the start of larger emotional waves, providing early alignment opportunities for observant traders.

Conclusion

Timing emotional waves transforms trading from **reactive guessing into informed participation**. By perceiving sentiment as a flowing, measurable force, traders can **enter, scale, and exit positions in harmony with the market's emotional energy**. This alignment reduces stress, enhances clarity, and improves long-term consistency in both observation and execution.

"The market's pulse is felt in the rise and fall of collective emotion; mastery is knowing when to ride and when to wait."

5.3 Pattern Recognition Through Rhythm

Markets are not purely random; they exhibit **repeating structures and rhythms** that emerge from collective behavior and emotional energy. Pattern recognition through rhythm involves **observing recurring oscillations, cycles, and micro-movements**, then interpreting them in context to anticipate potential market behavior. This skill transforms trading from mechanical reaction into **resonant participation with the market's energy**.

Understanding Rhythmic Patterns

- Rhythms exist at multiple scales: **micro-oscillations** (intraday or short-term fluctuations) and **macro-cycles** (weeks, months, or years).
- Repeating patterns are manifestations of **collective psychology** how traders respond to news, fear, greed, and expectation.
- By mapping these patterns, traders can **predict turning points, trend continuation, and potential reversals**.

Types of Rhythmic Patterns

1. **Oscillatory Patterns:** Repeated price swings around a mean level, reflecting short-term sentiment swings.

2. **Trend Waves:** Sustained directional movement punctuated by small retracements, indicating coordinated market alignment.

3. **Volatility Cycles:** Alternating periods of calm and intense activity, often corresponding to emotional waves.

4. **Fractal Structures:** Smaller patterns nested within larger cycles, showing self-similarity across timeframes.

Techniques for Recognizing Rhythm-Based Patterns

1. **Multi-Timeframe Observation:** - Examine patterns across intraday, daily, and weekly charts. - Confirm that micro-oscillations are consistent with macro-cycles to validate emerging patterns.

2. **Volume and Sentiment Correlation:** - Track volume spikes, order flow, and sentiment indicators. - Patterns reinforced by collective participation are more likely to signal true resonance.

3. **Wave Analysis:** - Identify the phase of the wave (accumulation, momentum, peak, dissipation) to anticipate the next movement. - Observe **amplitude and frequency changes** for early warning of trend shifts.

4. **Rhythmic Journaling:** - Maintain a record of observed patterns, market context, and emotional energy. - Over time, this builds a personal reference library of rhythmic signatures unique to specific markets or assets.

Practical Applications for Traders

- **Entry and exit timing:** Align trades with recurring rhythmic peaks and troughs rather than reacting impulsively.

- **Risk management:** Adjust exposure according to the amplitude of recognized waves. Larger waves allow for greater participation, smaller waves warrant caution.

- **Adaptive strategy:** Use rhythm recognition to anticipate market transitions before they fully manifest in price.

- **Refinement through reflection:** Regularly review rhythmic patterns observed versus outcomes to enhance predictive accuracy and intuitive alignment.

Examples of Rhythm-Based Pattern Recognition

- In equity markets, repeating intraday oscillations often signal accumulation before broader trend movements.
- Cryptocurrency markets frequently display fractal rhythm patterns, where micro-cycles within a 4-hour chart echo the behavior of weekly cycles, offering early alignment cues.
- Historical commodity markets show volatility cycles that coincide with seasonal or economic sentiment waves, providing anticipatory guidance for positioning.

Conclusion

Pattern recognition through rhythm is the practice of **seeing the invisible structure beneath price action**. It is a synthesis of observation, emotional awareness, and contextual understanding. Traders who master rhythmic recognition act with **timing, precision, and resonance**, moving in harmony with market energy rather than reacting to superficial noise.

"To read the market is to perceive its rhythm; to act in resonance is to dance with its pulse."

Part II

The Trader as Observer

Chapter 6

The Observer Effect in Trading

In physics, the observer effect describes how the very act of observing a system can influence its behavior. In markets, a similar principle applies: traders are not passive participants they are **active components of the system they study**. Every perception, decision, and action subtly shapes market behavior, creating a continuous feedback loop between observation and outcome.

This chapter explores how **mindset, perception, and conscious attention** influence trading results. We examine how beliefs and decisions collapse probabilities, how observation itself becomes participation, and how awareness of this dynamic can enhance both precision and intuition in trading.

By understanding the observer effect, traders learn to **align perception with action**, minimizing reactive impulses, and maximizing resonance with the underlying flow of market energy. This perspective transforms trading from a mechanistic endeavor into a **conscious dialogue with uncertainty**, where every observation carries the potential to shape both risk and opportunity.

6.1 Mindset Influences Outcomes

Trading is as much a reflection of the trader's mind as it is of external market forces. Your **mindset beliefs, expectations, and emotional state actively shapes the way you perceive opportunities and risks**, and by extension, the outcomes of your trades. Understanding this interplay is crucial for mastering the observer effect and trading in harmony with market energy.

The Role of Belief and Expectation

- Traders approach markets with **mental models**, assumptions, and prior experiences that influence interpretation.
- A belief in inevitable trends can lead to **confirmation bias**, reinforcing observations that match expectations and ignoring signals that contradict them.
- Conversely, cultivating an open and reflective mindset allows traders to **observe without distortion**, responding to signals objectively rather than emotionally.

Emotional State as a Market Lens

- Anxiety, fear, greed, and excitement distort perception, making some signals appear more significant than they are.
- A calm, observant, and centered mental state improves the **signal-to-noise ratio**, allowing subtle market cues to emerge clearly.
- Emotional regulation techniques mindfulness, controlled breathing, and reflective journaling enhance the trader's ability to see the market as it is, not as the mind projects it.

Cognitive Framing and Outcome Shaping

- How a trader frames a situation opportunity vs. threat, gain vs. loss directly influences **decision quality and timing**.
- Positive, growth-oriented framing encourages careful analysis and patience, while fear-driven framing often leads to **premature exits or overreactions**.
- Recognizing framing effects enables traders to consciously adjust their perception and **align decisions with true market conditions**.

Practical Strategies for Mindset Alignment

1. **Pre-Market Reflection:** - Begin each session by reviewing your mental and emotional state. - Ask: "Am I approaching the market with clarity or projection?"

2. **Mental Calibration Exercises:** - Short meditation or breathwork to center attention. - Journaling expectations and potential biases before trading to **increase self-awareness**.

3. **Observation Over Reaction:** - Focus on **seeing patterns and shifts objectively**, without immediate action. - Train the mind to separate perception from emotional response.

4. **Adaptive Reframing:** - Reframe setbacks as learning signals rather than personal failures. - Emphasize curiosity and inquiry over judgment to maintain clarity under pressure.

Examples in Practice

- A trader entering a volatile market with a calm, reflective mindset often notices subtle volume shifts and early trend indications that others miss.
- Conversely, a trader fueled by anxiety or fear may interpret ordinary fluctuations as catastrophic signals, resulting in **reactive, poorly-timed trades**.
- Historical market recoveries show that participants who maintained composure and detached observation during crises were better positioned to capitalize on subsequent trends.

Conclusion

Mindset is not merely a background factor it is a **primary driver of outcomes**. By cultivating clarity, emotional regulation, and reflective awareness, traders **shape their interaction with the market**, enhancing perception, timing, and decision quality. Mastery of mindset transforms the observer effect from a source of uncertainty into a **strategic advantage**, allowing traders to act in resonance with the market's underlying energy rather than being swept along by reactive impulses.

"The market mirrors the mind; calm observation creates clarity, and clarity guides aligned action."

6.2 Decisions Collapse Probabilities

In both quantum mechanics and behavioral finance, the act of decision-making has the power to **collapse a spectrum of potential outcomes into a single reality**. In trading, every choice you make whether to enter, exit, scale, or hold reduces a cloud of possibilities into a concrete result. Understanding this dynamic is essential for aligning your actions with market energy rather than reacting impulsively to uncertainty.

The Probabilistic Nature of Markets

- Before action, the market contains a **range of potential movements**, influenced by collective psychology, news, and random fluctuations.

- Traders interpret these possibilities and assign probabilities to different outcomes.
- While no one can predict the exact movement, **decisions interact with the market**, influencing the actual path the price takes.

The Observer Effect in Action

- Your **decision to act is an active observation** it participates in shaping the market.
- A large institutional order, or even a coordinated set of retail trades, can **shift supply-demand dynamics**, altering the likelihood of specific outcomes.
- Even in small-scale trades, your mental commitment to a position influences how you interpret subsequent signals, which in turn shapes further action.

Decision Timing and Probability Collapse

- Acting too early may **collapse probabilities prematurely**, locking you into a path without sufficient information.
- Acting too late may **miss the optimal collapse point**, leaving potential gains unclaimed.
- Mastery lies in **observing the emerging pattern, sensing the emotional and energetic state of the market, and choosing the moment to collapse probabilities consciously**.

Strategies for Conscious Probability Collapse

1. **Pre-Defined Decision Frameworks:** - Establish criteria for entries, exits, and scaling. - Reduces reactive impulses and ensures decisions collapse probabilities intentionally rather than haphazardly.

2. **Probability Mapping:** - Visualize multiple potential outcomes and their likelihoods. - Update probabilities as new data emerges, then act when alignment is optimal.

3. **Emotional Calibration:** - Observe internal reactions to market developments. - Avoid decisions dominated by fear, greed, or impatience, which collapse probabilities prematurely or incorrectly.

4. **Reflective Journaling:** - Record the thought process behind each decision and the market context. - Over time, this builds an intuitive sense for **when the timing of collapse aligns with resonance**.

Examples in Practice

- During the 2020 pandemic crash, traders who waited for micro-signals and confirmed emotional wave alignment entered positions at optimal probability collapse points, capturing significant upside.
- Conversely, traders acting impulsively on fear collapsed probabilities too early, entering or exiting positions at suboptimal levels, and often compounding losses.
- Cryptocurrency traders often experience similar dynamics: hesitation or premature action significantly changes realized outcomes, despite the same market "signals" being present.

Conclusion

Decisions do not occur in isolation they **interact with the market's probabilistic field**, collapsing possibilities into reality. Traders who cultivate awareness, timing, and emotional calibration **shape outcomes consciously**, turning uncertainty into a tool rather than a threat. By understanding how decisions collapse probabilities, one can move from reactive participation to **resonant, aligned action**, navigating markets with both insight and intentionality.

"Each choice is a key, unlocking one path from the infinite maze of possibilities. Choose with awareness, and the market bends to your resonance."

6.3 Observation as Active Participation

In markets, observing is not a passive act. Every glance at a chart, every analysis of price action, and every interpretation of sentiment **interacts with the system itself**, shaping outcomes in subtle and profound ways. This principle is the essence of the observer effect applied to trading: the act of watching is inseparable from participation.

Observation Shapes Perception and Action

- Traders inherently influence the market simply through **awareness and decision-making**.
- Observing patterns, trends, and micro-signals primes the mind for action, creating **cognitive momentum** that manifests in executed trades.

- By refining observation, traders can **align their attention with high-probability zones of market energy**, enhancing both timing and decision quality.

Active Observation Techniques

1. **Mindful Charting:** - Approach charts with a calm, reflective mindset. - Focus on **patterns, amplitude, and timing**, rather than emotional reactions to price movements.
2. **Sentiment Scanning:** - Observe the market's emotional undercurrents through news, social signals, or volume shifts. - Recognize that noting these signals **influences your own and, indirectly, collective market behavior**.
3. **Hypothesis Testing:** - Formulate potential scenarios based on observed signals. - Track how the market responds to these hypotheses, adjusting your perception in real time. - Each observation-feedback loop contributes to an **active shaping of probability outcomes**.
4. **Reflective Journaling:** - Document observations, emotional responses, and interpretations without immediate execution. - Over time, this trains the mind to observe **without impulsive action**, enhancing resonance with market rhythm.

Observation as a Form of Participation

- Every market participant is both **observer and influencer**.
- Even if no trade is executed, observation changes internal cognitive states, which in turn **affects future decisions** and, in aggregate with other traders, can influence market dynamics.
- Recognizing this dual role fosters **conscious awareness**, allowing traders to act with intention and clarity.

Practical Applications

- Use observation to **anticipate emerging trends** before they are fully reflected in price.
- Engage in deliberate **micro-observations** of volume, volatility, and sentiment, treating these as subtle signals of collective behavior.
- Balance observation with restraint; not all observations need immediate action. The value lies in **alignment with market flow**, not compulsive reaction.

Examples in Practice

- During the 2008 financial crisis, traders who spent time observing liquidity shifts and sentiment trends were able to **position strategically**, even without early trade execution.
- Cryptocurrency markets demonstrate how coordinated observation and action can create **self-reinforcing trends**, showing the power of active participation even at the retail level.
- Observers who journal and reflect on market micro-movements gain an **intuitive sense of rhythm**, often predicting turning points before they manifest clearly in price charts.

Conclusion

Observation is an **active, participatory act**. By recognizing the dual role of watcher and influencer, traders can develop **heightened awareness, emotional clarity, and timing precision**. Mastery of observation transforms the trading experience into a **resonant dialogue with the market**, where perception, intention, and action converge in harmony.

"To watch the market is not merely to see it is to participate consciously in the unfolding dance of collective behavior."

Chapter 7

Perception vs. Reality

Markets exist independently of any single trader's view, yet the way we perceive them profoundly shapes our decisions. What we see on charts, in news, or through social sentiment is filtered through **our cognitive lenses, biases, and emotional frameworks**. This creates a divergence between **market reality** the underlying flow of price and energy and **perceived reality**, the story our mind constructs around it.

This chapter explores the mechanisms that distort perception, including cognitive biases, narrative formation, and the human tendency to assign meaning where patterns may be coincidental. By understanding these perceptual filters, traders can **distinguish between objective signals and mental projections**, aligning decisions more closely with actual market dynamics rather than imagined trends.

Through reflective exercises and conceptual frameworks, we will examine how to **calibrate perception**, navigate cognitive pitfalls, and reconcile the difference between what the market is doing and what we think it is doing. Mastery of this alignment is critical for trading with clarity, precision, and resonance.

7.1 Cognitive Biases in Trading

Cognitive biases are the **systematic ways our minds deviate from rational judgment**, often without conscious awareness. In trading, these biases influence how we interpret market data, assess risk, and make decisions, creating a gap between **perceived reality** and the market's true dynamics. Recognizing and managing these biases is essential for aligning observation, analysis, and action with actual market conditions.

Key Cognitive Biases in Trading

- **Confirmation Bias:** The tendency to seek and favor information that supports existing beliefs while ignoring contradictory evidence. *Example: A trader convinced of an upward trend focuses only on bullish signals, overlooking early signs of reversal.*
- **Recency Bias:** Giving excessive weight to the most recent events or price movements. *Example: After a sudden market drop, a trader assumes prolonged decline, even if historical patterns suggest a rebound.*
- **Anchoring Bias:** Relying too heavily on initial information or price levels when making decisions. *Example: Fixating on a previous high as a "target," regardless of current market context.*
- **Loss Aversion:** The tendency to fear losses more than valuing equivalent gains, often leading to premature exits or holding losing positions. *Example: Avoiding a small stop-loss due to fear of realizing a loss, which allows a minor setback to escalate.*
- **Overconfidence:** Overestimating one's knowledge or predictive ability. *Example: Believing in the accuracy of a single indicator while ignoring contradictory market signals.*
- **Herding Bias:** Following the behavior of the majority without independent evaluation. *Example: Entering a crowded trade simply because others are doing so, rather than assessing underlying fundamentals or emotional resonance.*

The Impact of Bias on Market Interaction

- Biases distort perception, causing traders to misinterpret **micro-signals and emotional waves**.
- They amplify reactive behavior, leading to **missed opportunities or unnecessary risk exposure**.
- Biases can create feedback loops, where subjective perception reinforces collective market patterns, subtly altering price dynamics.

Strategies to Mitigate Cognitive Bias

1. **Self-Awareness and Reflection:** - Maintain a trading journal to note decisions, emotions, and assumptions. - Regularly review past trades to identify recurring biases.
2. **Predefined Rules and Frameworks:** - Use clear entry, exit, and risk management criteria to reduce impulsive decisions influenced by bias.

3. **Mindfulness and Emotional Calibration:** - Practice meditation or breathing exercises before trading sessions to reduce emotional distortion. - Train attention to distinguish **signal from noise** without judgment.
4. **Scenario Analysis:** - Consider multiple potential outcomes before committing to a trade. - Ask: "What am I missing? What evidence contradicts my view?"
5. **Peer Review and Feedback:** - Discuss trade ideas with trusted peers or mentors to counter personal blind spots. - Exposure to alternative perspectives reduces overconfidence and herding tendencies.

Conclusion

Cognitive biases are **inescapable aspects of human decision-making**, but awareness transforms them from hidden obstacles into manageable variables. By identifying biases, reflecting on patterns of thought, and applying structured mitigation strategies, traders can **bridge the gap between perception and reality**. Mastery of bias management enables observation and action that are **aligned, resonant, and adaptive**, enhancing both intuition and performance in complex market environments.

"The market does not lie, but our mind often interprets it through filters that cloud clarity. Awareness dissolves the distortion."

7.2 Narrative Creation and Interpretation

Humans are natural storytellers. We instinctively create narratives to make sense of complex, uncertain systems markets being among the most intricate. Narrative creation is the process of **assigning meaning and causality to price movements, sentiment shifts, and collective behavior**. While this can enhance understanding, it can also distort reality, leading traders to act on constructed stories rather than objective signals.

The Power of Narrative in Trading

- Narratives shape **attention, expectation, and risk perception**, influencing how traders interpret even neutral market data.
- A compelling story such as "this stock is a tech revolution" or "the market is headed for a crash" can drive collective behavior, **amplifying trends and volatility**.
- Narratives often **precede price movement**, as collective belief itself creates self-reinforcing patterns in markets.

Types of Market Narratives

1. **Fundamental Narratives:** Derived from economic, financial, or sectoral analysis. *Example: A company's innovation pipeline supports a bullish story.*

2. **Emotional Narratives:** Driven by fear, greed, hope, or despair. *Example: "Everyone is panicking, so it must be a buying opportunity."*

3. **Social Narratives:** Spread through media, forums, and peer discussion. *Example: Viral news influencing sentiment and triggering herd behavior.*

4. **Self-Reinforcing Narratives:** Created by traders' own beliefs and decisions, feeding back into the market. *Example: Overconfidence in a trend leads to repeated buying, validating the original narrative.*

Interpreting Narratives Without Being Trapped

- Distinguish between **story and signal**: narratives may explain price moves but are not always reliable predictors.
- Use narratives as **contextual lenses**, not as deterministic rules.
- Be aware of **personal narrative bias**: the stories we tell ourselves about why we bought or sold can reinforce cognitive biases.

Practical Strategies for Narrative Management

1. **Narrative Awareness:** - Explicitly identify the story you are hearing or telling yourself before taking action. - Ask: "Is this based on observable market behavior or my interpretation?"

2. **Multiple Perspectives:** - Consider alternative narratives for the same market movement. - Mapping several scenarios reduces the risk of **overcommitment to a single story**.

3. **Fact-Check Against Data:** - Compare narratives to actual price action, volume, and sentiment indicators. - Avoid letting the narrative alone dictate decisions.

4. **Journaling Narratives:** - Document the narrative behind each trade and review outcomes over time. - Identify patterns of overreaction or misinterpretation linked to recurring narrative traps.

Examples in Practice

- During the 2017–2018 cryptocurrency surge, narratives of "digital gold" and "mass adoption" drove enormous price swings, even when fundamental adoption metrics lagged. Traders who separated **narrative hype from objective signals** were better positioned to navigate volatility.

- In stock markets, investor fear narratives during the 2008 financial crisis led to panic selling, amplifying declines. Observant traders who saw the narrative as **collective emotion rather than reality** could identify early opportunities for strategic entry.
- Similarly, social narratives in meme stocks demonstrated how coordinated belief and storytelling can **create self-fulfilling trends**, emphasizing the dual role of perception and market action.

Conclusion

Narratives are powerful, unavoidable, and often self-reinforcing. The key is not to eliminate stories but to **observe, contextualize, and manage them consciously**, using them as a guide without letting them dictate action blindly. By mastering narrative interpretation, traders can **align perception with objective market reality**, enhancing both insight and decision quality.

"Markets tell stories, but it is the observer's clarity that separates signal from myth."

7.3 Meaning vs Price Mechanics

Trading is often a delicate balance between the **stories we assign to market events** and the **objective mechanics that drive price**. While meaning helps us interpret patterns, assign context, and navigate uncertainty, price mechanics are governed by **supply, demand, liquidity, and systemic flows**. Understanding the interplay between subjective interpretation and objective reality is crucial for aligned, resonant trading.

The Dual Layers of Market Perception

- **Meaning Layer:** - Constructed from cognitive interpretation, narrative, and emotional resonance. - Helps traders understand "why" markets move, creating a sense of order from chaos. - Example: Believing a stock is "undervalued" or "set to soar" based on perceived potential.
- **Price Mechanics Layer:** Objective forces that determine actual price changes: order flow, liquidity, volume, institutional participation, and algorithmic execution. - Independent of perception, these mechanics create the structure within which narratives play out. - Example: A large institutional sell order causes a sudden drop regardless of market sentiment.

Common Pitfalls

- Overemphasis on meaning can lead to **illusionary patterns** and impulsive trades.
- Ignoring price mechanics can result in **misreading microstructure signals**, such as volume spikes or order imbalances.
- Confusing correlation with causation amplifies errors narratives may seem predictive when in reality, **price moves according to objective mechanics**.

Integrating Meaning and Mechanics

1. **Observe Mechanics First:** - Analyze volume, liquidity, and order flow before interpreting emotional or narrative context.
2. **Layer Meaning Strategically:** - Use narratives, sentiment, and psychological insights to contextualize market behavior rather than dictate decisions.
3. **Check Resonance:** - Ask: Does my interpretation align with the underlying mechanics? - Avoid forcing a story to match price action; instead, let perception **resonate naturally with observed dynamics**.
4. **Reflective Practice:** - Journal both your interpretation and the mechanical data behind each trade. - Over time, this strengthens the ability to distinguish **signal (mechanics) from noise (meaning misalignment)**.

Practical Examples

- In the 2020 pandemic crash, traders who focused solely on narratives of fear or "rebound stories" often mistimed entries. Those who observed liquidity shifts, institutional positioning, and real-time order flow could **align narrative with mechanics**, capturing better outcomes.
- Cryptocurrency markets frequently demonstrate the divergence between hype-driven meaning and actual price mechanics. Coordinated social narratives can temporarily amplify moves, but ultimately, **mechanical factors such as exchanges, volume, and liquidity dictate the sustainability of trends**.
- In stock markets, retail sentiment may create short-term illusions of direction, but understanding **mechanics behind large trades, hedging, and algorithmic flows** allows traders to participate without being misled.

Conclusion

Meaning provides context, narrative, and emotional insight, while price mechanics deliver the objective structure of the market. The trader's skill lies in **integrating both layers**, using meaning to interpret dynamics without letting it override mechanics. By calibrating perception against the underlying system, traders can act with clarity, resonance, and strategic precision.

"Price moves according to mechanics, yet meaning shapes our response. Master both, and the market becomes a mirror of insight."

Chapter 8

Entanglement of Traders

Markets are not merely aggregations of individual actions they are **networks of intertwined perception, emotion, and decision-making**. Traders influence each other directly through transactions, indirectly through sentiment, and collectively through emergent patterns that transcend any single participant. This interconnectedness creates what can be called **market entanglement**: a phenomenon where beliefs, actions, and expectations propagate, resonate, and amplify across participants and assets.

In this chapter, we explore how collective cognition shapes market behavior, how correlation often masks deeper shared beliefs, and how psychological linkages extend across seemingly unrelated instruments. Understanding entanglement allows traders to recognize **hidden feedback loops**, anticipate the ripple effects of collective behavior, and make decisions that resonate with the underlying structure of market interactions.

Through conceptual frameworks, examples, and reflective exercises, this chapter will help you perceive the **subtle threads connecting trader psychology, market sentiment, and asset dynamics**, transforming trading from isolated actions into conscious participation in a living, entangled system.

8.1 Collective Cognition Across Markets

Markets are not simply the sum of individual decisions; they are **emergent systems shaped by collective cognition**. The aggregated beliefs, expectations, and emotional states of participants create patterns that influence price dynamics, volatility, and trend formation across entire markets. Understanding this collective mind allows traders to perceive **hidden alignments and systemic responses** that often precede observable price action.

Defining Collective Cognition

- **Shared Mental Models:** Traders often rely on common heuristics, narratives, and indicators. These shared frameworks create predictable responses to market events. Example: When a widely followed moving average is breached, many traders act in similar ways, reinforcing the move.

- **Emotional Resonance:** Fear, greed, and hope propagate across participants like waves, creating synchronized oscillations in buying and selling pressure. Example: Panic selling during a flash crash spreads rapidly because traders react to both price and the perceived sentiment of others.

- **Information Cascades:** Observing others' actions can reinforce beliefs, even without independent verification. Example: A sudden surge in retail buying of a stock may lead others to join, amplifying trends that originate from a few participants.

Mechanisms of Cross-Market Cognition

- **Correlation of Sentiment Across Assets:** Emotional and cognitive patterns often span multiple asset classes. A fear-driven equity sell-off may increase demand for safe-haven assets, demonstrating **intermarket entanglement**.

- **Information Flow and Social Amplification:** News, social media, and analyst commentary transmit perceptions rapidly, creating **instantaneous collective awareness** that affects prices across markets.

- **Reflexive Feedback Loops:** Collective expectations influence market outcomes, which in turn shape expectations anew. Example: Anticipated central bank moves can trigger preemptive trading, altering the very market dynamics the participants were expecting.

Practical Implications for Traders

1. **Observe Collective Behavior:** Track volume, sentiment indicators, and derivatives positioning to gauge **overall market cognition**.

2. **Identify Alignment Zones:** Recognize when multiple participants share beliefs or emotions that could **amplify moves**.

3. **Anticipate Ripple Effects:** Understand that **decisions in one market** may influence others through shared cognition and emotional entanglement.

4. **Maintain Independent Calibration:** While observing collective trends, avoid blind herding. Align your actions with **objective analysis and resonance with market flow**.

Examples in Practice

- During the 2008 financial crisis, the collective perception of systemic risk caused synchronized selling across equities, credit markets, and derivatives. Awareness of **cross-market cognition** allowed some traders to hedge effectively.
- In cryptocurrency markets, news or rumors often trigger synchronized movements across multiple coins, demonstrating **rapid propagation of collective belief**.
- Equity indices often move in tandem with macroeconomic announcements because the **aggregate interpretation of news by market participants** shapes correlated responses across sectors and geographies.

Conclusion

Recognizing collective cognition transforms trading from isolated decision-making into a **participatory awareness of market dynamics**. By observing shared mental models, emotional resonance, and reflexive feedback loops, traders can **anticipate systemic patterns**, align with emergent trends, and act in harmony with the collective rhythm of markets.

"Markets are not merely charts they are living reflections of a shared mind in constant motion."

8.2 Correlation, Causation, and Shared Belief

In complex markets, price movements often appear connected, but discerning the difference between **correlation and causation** is critical. Correlation measures the degree to which two variables move together, while causation implies a **direct influence of one variable on another**. Adding another layer, **shared belief** the collective perception and expectation of market participants can create apparent causal relationships where none exist.

Understanding these distinctions is vital for navigating the hidden dynamics of markets and avoiding false inferences that lead to poor decision-making.

Correlation vs. Causation

- **Correlation:** - Two assets moving together does not mean one causes the other's movement. - Example: Oil prices and airline stocks may show strong correlation, but multiple factors (fuel costs, investor sentiment, macroeconomic trends) contribute.

- **Causation:** - One event directly triggers another. - Example: A central bank interest rate hike can cause bond yields to rise; this is a clear mechanistic influence.

- **Mistaking Correlation for Causation:** - Traders often assume a relationship exists purely because two variables move together temporarily. - This can lead to **overconfidence, misaligned trades, and unexpected exposure**.

The Role of Shared Belief

- Markets are shaped not just by fundamentals but by **collective perception**. - Example: If traders believe a technology stock will rise, their buying actions can **create a self-fulfilling price movement**.

- Shared belief can create **apparent causal links** across unrelated assets: - Example: During a market-wide risk-off event, equities and commodities may drop together not because one causes the other, but because **investors share a fear-driven worldview**.

- Understanding shared belief allows traders to differentiate between **mechanical causation** and **psychological amplification**.

Practical Strategies for Traders

1. **Identify True Causal Drivers:** - Focus on fundamental forces and price mechanics to determine what actually moves the market.

2. **Analyze Correlations Critically:** - Examine the **duration, consistency, and context** of correlated moves before assuming predictive power.

3. **Map Shared Beliefs:** - Observe sentiment indicators, social media, news narratives, and market positioning to understand collective expectations. - Determine when a movement is **belief-driven rather than fundamentally causal**.

4. **Use Reflexive Awareness:** - Recognize that your own beliefs contribute to shared market perception. - Avoid reinforcing false correlations through reactive trading.

Examples in Practice

- **2008 Financial Crisis:** Mortgage-backed securities and banking equities moved downward together. While correlated, some moves were caused by liquidity stress (causation), others by panic-driven shared belief (self-reinforcing correlation).

- **Cryptocurrency Markets:** Bitcoin and altcoins often move in tandem. While some causation exists (Bitcoin price leading sentiment), much of the correlation is **driven by collective belief** and herd psychology.
- **Tech Stock Surges:** When a narrative about "sector dominance" spreads, multiple unrelated tech stocks can rise simultaneously, **creating correlation without fundamental causation**.

Conclusion

Correlation, causation, and shared belief are **distinct yet intertwined forces** in markets. Traders who recognize the difference between mechanical causation, coincidental correlation, and belief-driven amplification can **navigate complex market interactions with clarity**. Mastering this distinction enables observation of **true market dynamics**, minimizes misinterpretation, and enhances the alignment of perception and action.

> *"The market whispers patterns; wisdom lies in discerning whether they speak of reality, coincidence, or collective belief."*

8.3 Psychological Linkages Across Assets

Markets are not isolated silos; they are **interconnected networks of perception, emotion, and expectation**. Traders' psychological states often propagate across multiple assets, creating patterns that appear correlated, even when fundamental links are weak or absent. These cross-asset psychological connections what we term **psychological linkages** can significantly influence price dynamics, risk perception, and opportunity recognition.

Understanding Cross-Asset Psychology

- **Emotional Contagion:** - Fear, greed, and euphoria in one market can spill over into others. - Example: A sudden equity sell-off may trigger safe-haven buying in gold or government bonds, even if fundamentals have not changed.
- **Cognitive Bias Propagation:** - Traders often apply the same interpretive framework across different assets. - Example: Overconfidence in technology stocks may lead to similar bullish assumptions in unrelated sectors like biotech or AI, amplifying perceived trends.
- **Herding Across Markets:** - Collective belief in one market can encourage imitative behavior in others, creating **synchronous moves**.

- Example: Cryptocurrency gains often influence speculative behavior in related digital assets and tokens.

Mechanisms of Psychological Linkage

1. **Narrative Spillover:** - A compelling story in one asset class can affect sentiment in others. - Example: The narrative of "digital transformation" in tech stocks can drive investment flows into tech ETFs, software, and cloud infrastructure.

2. **Global Sentiment Waves:** - Macroeconomic or geopolitical events create waves of sentiment that ripple through multiple markets simultaneously. - Example: Interest rate hikes by central banks affect equities, currencies, and commodities in a linked psychological response.

3. **Reflexive Feedback Loops:** - Traders' reactions in one market feed back into others, creating **emotional amplification**. - Example: Fear of losses in equities may lead to liquidation of high-risk debt instruments, which then reinforces equity declines.

Implications for Trading

- **Observe Sentiment Across Assets:** - Track correlations not just statistically but psychologically. Emotional states often **precede mechanical movements**.

- **Identify Propagation Paths:** - Recognize which assets are likely to influence others due to shared trader perception, liquidity flows, or market narratives.

- **Adjust Positioning Strategically:** - Exploit cross-asset linkages to anticipate **secondary reactions** and hedge or amplify trades accordingly.

- **Maintain Mental Calibration:** - Avoid being unconsciously pulled by linked sentiment; use journaling, reflection, and signal filtering to **separate resonance from noise**.

Examples in Practice

- During global crises, like the 2020 pandemic, **fear-driven equity sell-offs** were mirrored in commodities, currencies, and bond markets. Traders who understood psychological linkages could anticipate safe-haven flows and capitalize on them.

- In cryptocurrency markets, Bitcoin price surges often lead to coordinated movement in altcoins due to **collective trader sentiment and belief structures**, rather than fundamental changes in each asset.

- Equity indices in different countries often move together following **global narratives** like trade policy shifts or interest rate decisions, reflecting **psychological linkages** rather than direct economic causation.

Conclusion

Psychological linkages across assets highlight the **interconnected nature of markets** at the level of perception and emotion. Traders who recognize these linkages gain an **early awareness of cascading effects**, anticipate emergent trends, and can navigate volatility with greater clarity. By observing how sentiment, belief, and expectation travel across markets, one develops the capacity to **align actions with collective dynamics**, rather than reacting solely to isolated price movements.

"Markets are a web of interlinked minds; understanding the threads between assets transforms chaos into discernible rhythm."

Chapter 9

Superposition and Indecision

Markets often exist in a state of **uncertainty**, where multiple potential outcomes coexist simultaneously. Traders, in turn, oscillate between conflicting emotions, expectations, and decisions. This phenomenon can be understood through the lens of **superposition**, borrowed conceptually from quantum theory: multiple possibilities exist at once, and observation or action collapses potential outcomes into reality.

In this chapter, we explore how **fear and hope oscillate**, creating cycles of indecision, hesitation, and impulsive action. We will examine how indecision itself can serve as a **valuable signal**, revealing subtle shifts in market sentiment before they manifest in price. Finally, we discuss how to recognize these **quantum-like states in trader psychology**, allowing for aligned action that resonates with underlying market energy rather than reacting reflexively to apparent noise.

Through conceptual frameworks, reflective exercises, and practical examples, this chapter aims to equip traders with the ability to perceive, interpret, and act upon the **hidden potentials** that exist in every moment of market uncertainty.

9.1 Fear-Hope Oscillation

Every trader experiences a constant ebb and flow between **fear and hope**, two of the most powerful emotional drivers in markets. These opposing forces do not merely exist in isolation; they interact, overlap, and oscillate, creating a dynamic emotional landscape that profoundly influences decision-making, timing, and perception of risk.

The Nature of the Oscillation

- **Fear:** - Arises from uncertainty, potential loss, or perceived vulnerability. - Heightens vigilance, narrows focus, and often triggers defensive or reactive behavior. - Example: A sudden price drop can provoke immediate selling, sometimes amplifying downward momentum.
- **Hope:** - Emerges from anticipation of gains, opportunity, or favorable outcomes. - Encourages proactive positioning, calculated risk-taking, and creative problem-solving. - Example: Traders may increase exposure when sensing a rebound, occasionally overestimating the probability of success.
- **Oscillation:** - Traders rarely remain in a single emotional state; fear and hope alternate in cycles, sometimes rapidly within minutes or seconds. - This oscillation can create hesitation, indecision, or impulsive moves depending on amplitude and alignment with market flow.

Measuring Emotional Cycles

- **Amplitude:** - The intensity of emotional swings high amplitude indicates extreme reactions, low amplitude suggests calm resilience.
- **Frequency:** - How quickly traders move between fear and hope rapid oscillations can create noise, while slower cycles often reveal deeper sentiment shifts.
- **Phase Alignment:** - Synchronization of emotional cycles across traders can amplify market moves. When fear and hope resonate collectively, trends strengthen; when desynchronized, markets appear choppy.

Practical Implications for Traders

1. **Awareness of Emotional States:** - Recognize your own fear-hope cycles and how they influence perception, entry, and exit decisions.
2. **Observe Collective Oscillation:** - Track market-wide sentiment indicators, volume, and price patterns to gauge the dominant emotional rhythm.
3. **Leverage Oscillation as Signal:** - Extreme fear can signal potential buying opportunities; extreme hope may indicate caution. - Use emotional extremes as **contrarian indicators**, but only when aligned with structural market mechanics.
4. **Maintain Emotional Calibration:** - Journaling, mindfulness, and reflective exercises help modulate oscillation amplitude, preventing overreaction or paralysis.

Examples in Practice

- **2008 Financial Crisis:** Fear peaked during liquidity crunches, while intermittent hope surged during bailout announcements, creating oscillating market swings that astute traders could anticipate.
- **Cryptocurrency Markets:** Bitcoin often demonstrates rapid oscillations of fear and hope sharp dips provoke panic selling, followed by speculative optimism during rebounds.
- **Equity Market Corrections:** Short-term fear-hope cycles within intraday price movements can signal **microtrends** that are exploitable for scalping or swing trading strategies.

Conclusion

Fear and hope are not just emotions; they are **dynamic signals** that encode collective trader psychology. By observing oscillations within yourself and across the market, traders gain a **window into the underlying emotional frequency** driving price movements. Mastering the awareness and alignment with these cycles allows for **calibrated, resonant decision-making**, turning emotional oscillation from a source of noise into a tool for insight.

"The market moves not only with money, but with the rhythm of our collective fear and hope. To see it is to begin to ride it."

9.2 Harnessing Indecision as Signal

Indecision in markets is often dismissed as noise or uncertainty, but in reality, it carries **valuable informational content**. When traders hesitate, oscillate, or delay action, it reflects an underlying **tension between competing forces** fear vs. hope, risk vs. reward, or conflicting narratives. Recognizing and interpreting these moments of indecision can provide early signals of **potential turning points, consolidations, or emergent trends**.

The Nature of Market Indecision

- **Behavioral Roots:** - Indecision arises when market participants are uncertain about valuation, timing, or external catalysts. - Example: A stock may hover near a key support level as buyers and sellers assess risk before committing.
- **Oscillatory Dynamics:** - The market may swing within a narrow range, reflecting the tug-of-war between bullish and bearish sentiment.

- These oscillations often precede **breakouts or breakdowns**, making them a precursor to movement.

- **Psychological Significance:** - Indecision represents a collective **pause in commitment**, highlighting points of maximum uncertainty and potential leverage for attentive traders.

Reading Indecision as a Signal

1. **Identify Consolidation Zones:** - Price ranges with low volatility often indicate indecision. These zones can reveal **support and resistance** or points where market sentiment is in equilibrium.

2. **Observe Volume Patterns:** - Low or fluctuating volume during indecision indicates hesitation. Sudden spikes in volume may signal that a resolution is imminent.

3. **Track Sentiment Indicators:** - Social media, news sentiment, and option positioning can reveal **contradictory beliefs**, which manifest as indecision in price.

4. **Monitor Emotional Oscillation:** - Cross-reference fear-hope cycles with indecision periods; extreme oscillations often precede decisive moves.

Practical Applications

- **Anticipating Breakouts:** - Narrow, indecisive ranges frequently precede strong directional moves. Traders can position **preemptively**, either through options, partial entries, or layered scaling strategies.

- **Contrarian Opportunities:** - When the market hesitates near extremes of sentiment, indecision can highlight areas where **contrarian positioning** may yield higher probability outcomes.

- **Risk Management:** - Recognizing indecision prevents premature commitment. Traders can **wait for clarity or partial confirmation**, reducing exposure to false moves.

- **Reflective Observation:** - Journaling indecision points helps calibrate your perception of market uncertainty, improving the ability to detect subtle shifts in collective psychology.

Examples in Practice

- **Equity Consolidation:** - Before the S&P 500 breakout in early 2013, the index spent weeks oscillating within a narrow range. Traders who recognized the indecision as a potential signal were able to anticipate and align with the subsequent trend.

- **Cryptocurrency Ranges:** - Bitcoin often experiences multi-day periods of indecision around psychological price levels (e.g., $20,000). These zones provide cues for **volatility expansion and breakout strategies**.

- **Forex Market Stalemates:** - Currency pairs frequently hover near major support or resistance with indecision reflected in oscillating sentiment indicators, hinting at upcoming volatility upon resolution.

Conclusion

Indecision is not a void; it is a **latent signal of market potential**. By learning to observe hesitation, consolidation, and oscillation, traders can transform moments of uncertainty into **anticipatory insights**, allowing them to act with alignment rather than reaction. Mastering the art of interpreting indecision cultivates **attunement to the hidden rhythm of markets**, bridging perception and informed action.

"In the stillness of indecision, the market whispers its next move; those who listen can act before the world decides."

9.3 Recognizing Quantum States in Trader Psychology

Markets, much like quantum systems, often exist in **superposed states** multiple potential outcomes coexist until a decisive observation or action occurs. Traders, as active participants in these systems, also experience internal superposition: simultaneous possibilities, conflicting intuitions, and dual emotional states. Recognizing these **quantum-like states in psychology** is essential for developing clarity, patience, and resonance with the market's underlying energy.

The Concept of Psychological Superposition

- **Multiple Possibilities Coexist:** - A trader may simultaneously anticipate both bullish and bearish scenarios. - For example, observing a support level may trigger hope for a rebound, while looming macroeconomic risks generate fear.

- **Indecision as Superposition:** - Hesitation and oscillation between choices represent a **mental superposition**, where the trader has not yet collapsed the probabilities into action.

- **Observation Collapses Potential:** - In quantum analogy, taking an action placing an order, entering or exiting a position **collapses multiple possibilities into one realized outcome.** - Awareness of this process allows traders to act deliberately rather than reactively.

Identifying Quantum States in Yourself

1. **Emotional Multiplicity:** - Notice when fear, hope, doubt, and optimism coexist. These conflicting emotions often signal a state of **psychological superposition**.
2. **Cognitive Tension:** - When your analysis supports multiple scenarios equally, you are experiencing a **mental probability cloud**, requiring careful observation before committing.
3. **Behavioral Oscillation:** - Rapid shifts in micro-decisions hovering over entries, canceling orders, or adjusting stop-loss levels repeatedly reflect a **collapsed state that has not yet stabilized.**

Practical Application in Trading

- **Awareness and Journaling:** - Record moments when you feel pulled in multiple directions. This builds recognition of recurring quantum states and helps **calibrate decision-making**.
- **Deliberate Observation Before Action:** - Avoid impulsive collapse of probabilities. Instead, **observe, gather data, and sense market resonance** before acting.
- **Use Superposition as Insight:** - Conflicting intuitions often highlight areas of **high market tension**, which can precede significant moves. Treat them as **informational signals** rather than obstacles.
- **Align Mind with Market Energy:** - By recognizing your own superposed mental states, you can **synchronize your action with the market's latent potential**, rather than forcing resolution prematurely.

Examples in Practice

- **Equity Range-Bound Trading:** - During consolidation phases, traders often feel simultaneously bullish and bearish. Those who recognize this superposition can **position cautiously, scaling in gradually**, rather than overcommitting.
- **Cryptocurrency Swings:** - Rapid oscillations in price create a state where the market itself is superposed. Traders who sense this latent energy before committing can **capitalize on breakout moves** while managing risk.

- **Macro Event Anticipation:** - Ahead of central bank announcements, conflicting expectations coexist in all markets. Awareness of your internal superposition helps maintain **composure and alignment**, avoiding emotional overreaction.

Conclusion

Recognizing quantum states in trader psychology transforms indecision and internal conflict into a **source of insight rather than a liability**. By observing superposed emotions, cognitions, and potential outcomes, traders can act with **measured intention**, aligning their decisions with the **latent dynamics of the market**. Mastery of these states enables a higher level of **resonant awareness**, where perception, intuition, and action converge harmoniously.

"In the superposition of doubt and anticipation lies the hidden frequency of opportunity; the mindful trader listens, waits, and then collapses possibilities into aligned action."

Chapter 10

Time Distortion in Trading

Time in trading is rarely experienced as linear. Seconds can stretch into hours during moments of intense emotion, and hours can collapse into a blur when the mind is aligned with market flow. This chapter explores how **psychological and emotional states distort perception of time**, how flow states accelerate awareness, and how traders can **manage temporal pressure** to act with clarity and precision.

We will examine the interplay between **emotion, cognition, and temporal perception**, revealing how fear, hope, and stress can warp judgment and reaction times. By understanding these distortions, traders can harness **flow states**, recognize accelerated or decelerated perception, and structure decisions to capitalize on critical moments while maintaining composure.

Through practical exercises, reflective techniques, and real-world examples, this chapter equips traders to navigate the **elasticity of time in markets**, transforming temporal distortion from a source of error into a tool for insight and alignment.

10.1 Emotional Influence on Time Perception

In trading, our experience of time is rarely objective. Emotions particularly fear, hope, excitement, and stress can **expand or contract the perception of time**, altering decision-making, risk assessment, and execution. Recognizing these distortions is essential for aligning perception with reality and avoiding impulsive or delayed actions.

How Emotions Affect Time Perception

- **Fear: Time Dilation** - During moments of fear or anxiety, traders often experience time as **slowing down**. Each tick, candle, or quote can feel prolonged, creating over-analysis and hesitation. - Example:

Watching a position drop rapidly can make seconds feel like minutes, leading to **paralysis or panic selling**.

- **Hope and Anticipation: Time Compression** - When anticipating gains or opportunities, time seems to **accelerate**. Important cues may pass unnoticed, and decisions may be rushed. - Example: Waiting for a breakout while expecting a surge can make the period leading up to it feel short, prompting premature entries or over-leveraging.
- **Stress and Cognitive Load** - High stress from market volatility or personal pressure distorts attention, making time perception inconsistent. Traders may misjudge durations, holding periods, or reaction windows.

Implications for Trading

1. **Reaction Timing:** - Misperception of time can lead to early or delayed execution, causing slippage, missed opportunities, or amplified losses.
2. **Risk Assessment:** - Emotional expansion of time (fear) exaggerates potential losses; contraction (hope) exaggerates potential gains. Awareness allows **objective calibration of position size and risk tolerance**.
3. **Decision Quality:** - Time distortion affects cognitive processing. By recognizing it, traders can **pause, breathe, and structure decisions**, ensuring alignment with market reality.

Strategies to Mitigate Temporal Distortion

- **Mindfulness and Self-Observation:** - Regularly check your emotional state and note whether time feels accelerated or slowed. Awareness alone reduces bias in perception.
- **Journaling and Reflection:** - Record emotional intensity and perceived time during trades. Over time, patterns emerge, allowing predictive awareness of when perception may be distorted.
- **Structured Decision Frameworks:** - Use checklists, pre-defined rules, and timers to **anchor perception**, preventing emotions from distorting execution.
- **Breathing and Micro-Pauses:** - Short, deliberate pauses reset attention and perception, helping traders **restore temporal alignment** during high-pressure moments.

Examples in Practice

- **Flash Crashes:** - During rapid market collapses, fear-induced time dilation leads to exaggerated reactions, such as panic selling, which may amplify volatility.
- **Breakout Anticipation:** - Traders waiting for a bullish breakout may feel time compressing due to hope and excitement, causing them to **enter too early or over-leverage**.
- **High-Frequency Trading Observations:** - Even professional traders in fast markets experience subjective time distortion, demonstrating that emotional influence on temporal perception is universal.

Conclusion

Time is not fixed in the mind of the trader it is **elastic, shaped by emotional currents**. By observing and understanding how fear, hope, and stress warp temporal perception, traders can **calibrate their attention, actions, and risk**, turning a potential vulnerability into a strategic advantage. Mastery of emotional time perception allows for more deliberate, aligned, and resonant trading, even in the most turbulent markets.

"In the market, seconds can stretch into eternity or vanish in a heartbeat; the skill is not in rushing time, but in moving with its hidden rhythm."

10.2 Flow States and Accelerated Awareness

Flow is a state of **total immersion, heightened focus, and effortless action**, where perception and execution converge seamlessly. In trading, flow allows individuals to process complex information rapidly, anticipate market movements intuitively, and respond with clarity even under pressure. This section explores how flow accelerates awareness, enhances decision-making, and creates a sense of temporal expansion or compression that aligns with market rhythm.

Characteristics of Flow in Trading

- **Intense Focus:** - Attention narrows on the task at hand, minimizing distractions and irrelevant stimuli. - Traders in flow can perceive subtle signals micro-patterns, emotional micro-signals, or minor volume shifts that would normally go unnoticed.

- **Effortless Action:** - Decisions and executions occur smoothly, without hesitation. Actions feel automatic yet informed, integrating intuition with analysis.
- **Heightened Awareness:** - Sensory and cognitive perception is amplified. Market rhythms, trends, and emerging anomalies become more apparent, enhancing predictive capabilities.
- **Distorted Sense of Time:** - Flow often compresses or expands subjective time, making prolonged periods of intense observation feel instantaneous, or brief windows appear elongated, aiding precise execution.

Triggers for Flow in Trading

1. **Challenge-Skill Balance:** - Flow emerges when the complexity of the market matches the trader's skill level neither overwhelming nor under-stimulating.
2. **Clear Goals and Immediate Feedback:** - Well-defined objectives (e.g., monitoring a breakout zone or managing a position) and instant feedback from price action help maintain immersion.
3. **Minimized Self-Consciousness:** - Letting go of ego-driven fears or attachment to outcomes allows the trader to respond to the market without interference from internal narrative.
4. **Adaptive Attention:** - Shifting focus dynamically between macro trends and micro-signals supports sustained engagement with the evolving market environment.

Practical Strategies to Enter Flow

- **Pre-Trade Calibration:** - Mindfulness, breathing, or short meditation exercises before trading prepare the mind for heightened focus and emotional equilibrium.
- **Structured Observation:** - Use checklists, watchlists, and pre-defined alert systems to reduce cognitive clutter, freeing attention to detect subtle market signals.
- **Micro-Routines for Alignment:** - Small rituals reviewing charts, noting emotional states, or visualizing outcomes help trigger a consistent flow state.
- **Journaling and Reflection:** - Post-trade analysis reinforces awareness of the conditions that led to flow, helping replicate optimal states in future sessions.

Examples in Practice

- **Equity Scalping:** - Experienced scalpers often describe "seeing the market in slow motion" while executing trades rapidly, reflecting accelerated awareness.
- **Forex Trading:** - Flow enables traders to integrate price action, macro news, and order book dynamics simultaneously, allowing anticipatory positioning.
- **Algorithmic Overlay and Human Intuition:** - When combining manual oversight with automated strategies, flow allows traders to **interpret deviations from expected algorithmic behavior** in real-time, capturing edge opportunities.

Conclusion

Flow is not just a psychological state; it is a **resonant alignment of mind and market**. By cultivating the conditions for flow, traders can accelerate awareness, perceive subtle cues, and act decisively while maintaining emotional and cognitive coherence. Mastery of flow transforms trading from reactive activity into a **synchronized, resonant practice**, where time distortion becomes a tool for insight rather than a challenge.

> *"In flow, the market speaks directly to your awareness; you do not chase it you move with it, sensing its hidden rhythm and responding with effortless clarity."*

10.3 Managing Temporal Pressure

Temporal pressure in trading arises when **decisions must be made quickly**, often under uncertainty and high emotional intensity. It can distort perception, trigger reactive behavior, and amplify mistakes. Effective management of temporal pressure transforms stress into clarity, allowing traders to act deliberately, in alignment with market rhythms.

Sources of Temporal Pressure

- **Market Volatility:** - Rapid price movements create the perception that every second counts, increasing cognitive load and emotional arousal.
- **Opportunity Scarcity:** - When potential trades appear limited, traders may feel compelled to act quickly, risking premature or misaligned decisions.

- **External Expectations:** - Pressure from performance targets, clients, or social comparison can intensify urgency, leading to **reactionary trading**.
- **Internal Emotional States:** - Fear, excitement, or overconfidence amplifies the perception of temporal scarcity, skewing judgment and risk assessment.

Psychological Impact of Temporal Pressure

- **Reduced Cognitive Bandwidth:** - High pressure compresses mental resources, leading to **simplified heuristics** and potential errors.
- **Impaired Pattern Recognition:** - Rapid decision-making can obscure subtle market signals and emotional micro-patterns that would normally inform judgment.
- **Emotional Hijacking:** - Strong stress responses may override reasoned analysis, triggering impulsive entries, exits, or over-leveraging.

Strategies to Manage Temporal Pressure

1. **Pre-Defined Decision Frameworks:** - Establish **clear rules for entries, exits, and risk management** ahead of time. These frameworks reduce the need for split-second judgments under stress.
2. **Micro-Pacing:** - Break complex decisions into **small, sequential steps**. Focusing on one micro-action at a time reduces cognitive overload.
3. **Mindfulness and Breath Anchoring:** - Simple breathing exercises or short mindfulness pauses help **regulate heart rate and perception of urgency**, restoring mental clarity.
4. **Temporal Visualization:** - Mentally map market events onto a broader temporal horizon, reminding yourself that **not every tick requires immediate action**.
5. **Journaling and Reflection:** - Review past moments of high temporal pressure to identify patterns in emotional response and refine strategies for future situations.

Practical Applications

- **Scalping and Day Trading:** - Traders can pre-plan **decision windows** for rapid sequences, using timers or alerts to mitigate hasty reactions.

- **Swing and Position Trading:** - Recognizing that temporal pressure is often self-imposed, traders can **step back**, allowing natural market movement to provide clarity before committing.
- **High-Impact News Events:** - During economic releases or earnings announcements, pressure peaks. Using structured frameworks and micro-pacing ensures **aligned responses rather than emotional overreaction**.

Conclusion

Temporal pressure is inevitable in markets, but it need not dictate outcomes. By understanding its sources, recognizing its psychological impact, and implementing structured mitigation strategies, traders can **preserve clarity, make deliberate choices, and maintain emotional balance**. Mastering temporal pressure transforms apparent urgency into a **strategic tool**, enabling aligned action, better risk management, and resonance with the market's rhythm.

"Time may feel compressed, but clarity expands it; in managing temporal pressure, the trader finds the rhythm of decisive, aligned action."

Chapter 11

Emotional & Cognitive Architecture

Chapter 12

Energy Signatures of Price Moves

Price movements in markets are not merely mechanical; they are **manifestations of collective emotion, attention, and intent**. Just as physical systems have energy signatures patterns that reveal underlying dynamics markets carry **emotional and cognitive energy** that shapes the trajectory of price action. Recognizing these signatures allows traders to sense the **latent potential** behind every move, rather than merely reacting to past data.

This chapter introduces the concept of **energy signatures**, small yet powerful indicators embedded in price, volume, and market behavior. We will explore how to detect **micro-moments of resonance**, identify **emotional leading indicators**, and recognize **subtle shifts in trend** before they become obvious to the broader market.

By training awareness to these energy patterns, traders can develop a **resonant understanding of price dynamics**, anticipate turning points, and align actions with the market's underlying rhythm rather than its surface noise.

Through practical examples, reflective exercises, and conceptual frameworks, this chapter equips traders to interpret the **emotional and energetic undercurrents** that drive market behavior, transforming observation into actionable insight.

12.1 Micro-Moments of Resonance

Markets pulse with subtle fluctuations that reflect the **collective emotional and cognitive state** of participants. These fluctuations often occur in **micro-moments of resonance**, brief intervals where trader perception, sentiment, and market action align in a coherent, amplifying pattern. Recognizing these moments provides insight into **emerging trends, reversals,**

and shifts in momentum before they become widely apparent.

Understanding Resonance in Markets

- **Definition of Micro-Resonance:** - A micro-moment of resonance is a short-lived interval during which **market participants' actions reinforce each other**, creating amplified energy in price movements. - Example: A cluster of rapid buy orders in a low-volume stock can trigger a small, sudden upward movement that signals early accumulation by informed traders.
- **Emotional and Cognitive Alignment:** - These moments occur when trader emotions such as confidence, fear, or anticipation synchronize, creating **coherent micro-movements**. - They are often invisible in standard charts but detectable through **volume spikes, order flow imbalances, or sudden volatility compression**.

Identifying Micro-Moments

1. **Price-Volume Confluence:** - A brief surge in volume accompanying a small price movement often indicates that collective attention is focusing in a **coherent direction**.
2. **Volatility Compression and Release:** - Periods of low volatility followed by sharp micro-movements can signal **latent energy being released**, often preceding larger trends.
3. **Pattern Repetition:** - Recurrent micro-patterns such as rapid small candles, order book imbalances, or clustered trade executions suggest **resonance points** forming in the market.

Practical Observations

- **High-Frequency Monitoring:** - Traders observing **short timeframes or tick data** can detect these micro-moments and anticipate larger price moves.
- **Integration with Broader Context:** - Micro-resonance is most meaningful when interpreted within the **macro trend, market sentiment, and sector behavior**. A small burst of energy in isolation may not indicate a sustained move.
- **Emotional Calibration:** - Recognizing micro-moments requires **mindful attention and emotional stability**, as rapid movements can trigger premature reactions.

Exercises for Traders

- Monitor short-term charts (1-5 min) for **clusters of small price movements** and note accompanying volume changes. Reflect on emotional response during these intervals.
- Compare these micro-moments with subsequent price action over longer timeframes to understand which **resonances preceded significant moves**.
- Practice observing without immediate reaction. This trains the mind to **distinguish true resonance from noise**.

Conclusion

Micro-moments of resonance are the **hidden pulses** of the market. They reveal the synchronization of trader psychology and market behavior, providing early insight into potential trends and shifts. By training attention to detect these subtle signals, traders can **anticipate movements, align with market energy**, and act from a position of awareness rather than reaction.

"The market whispers before it roars; those who perceive the whisper in its micro-resonance move with foresight rather than hindsight."

12.2 Emotional Leading Indicators

Markets are more than charts and numbers; they are **collective expressions of human emotion, expectation, and perception**. Emotional leading indicators are **subtle precursors** embedded in market behavior that signal the **emerging sentiment** of traders before it fully materializes in price. By observing these indicators, traders can anticipate potential trends, reversals, or accelerations, gaining a crucial edge in aligning with the market's energy.

Types of Emotional Leading Indicators

1. **Volume Anomalies:** - Sudden spikes in trading volume, especially when price moves are minimal, often indicate **latent emotional energy**. - Example: A series of small buy orders in a low-liquidity stock can reveal **early accumulation driven by optimism or confidence**.

2. **Volatility Shifts:** - Compression or expansion of volatility can reflect collective anticipation, uncertainty, or anxiety. - Low volatility followed by clustered activity may precede a **breakout**, signaling the emotional tension being released.

3. **Order Flow Imbalances:** - Disproportionate bid-ask pressure can reveal **dominant sentiment** among active traders. - For instance, persistent aggressive buying despite minor price increases can indicate **underlying bullish conviction**.

4. **News and Social Sentiment:** - Emotional responses to news, rumors, or social media discussions often **lead actual market reactions**. - Tracking sentiment shifts can uncover **early shifts in collective expectation**.

5. **Behavioral Micro-Patterns:** - Recurrent micro-oscillations in short-term charts often reflect **fear-hope oscillation** among traders. - These micro-patterns act as **psychological early-warning signals** of possible trend continuation or reversal.

Detecting and Interpreting Emotional Indicators

- **Observation and Calibration:** - Develop awareness by **monitoring micro-movements, clustering of trades, and sudden shifts in volume or bid-ask pressure**. - Pair observation with journaling to **correlate emotional cues with subsequent price behavior**.

- **Contextual Analysis:** - Emotional indicators must be interpreted relative to **broader market context, macro trends, and asset-specific behavior**. - A volume spike in isolation may be noise; when aligned with a macro sentiment trend, it becomes a **leading signal**.

- **Quantitative Tools:** - Techniques such as **order book imbalance metrics, sentiment scoring, and volatility skew analysis** can quantify emotional pressure, giving structure to qualitative observation.

Practical Applications

- Identify **early trend initiation** by observing subtle shifts in volume and micro-price movements.

- Anticipate **reversals or pullbacks** when emotional indicators diverge from prevailing trends.

- Integrate emotional leading indicators into **resonant trading frameworks**, combining intuition, observation, and structured decision-making.

Exercises for Traders

- Track a market instrument for a week, noting micro-volume spikes, bid-ask imbalances, and news-driven sentiment shifts.

- Compare observed signals with subsequent price action to identify which indicators **consistently led meaningful moves**.

- Practice **non-reactive observation**, recording emotional cues without immediately trading, to strengthen pattern recognition and awareness.

Conclusion

Emotional leading indicators are the **pulse points of market psychology**. They allow traders to perceive **latent energy and emerging sentiment** before it manifests fully in price action. By cultivating sensitivity to these indicators, aligning observation with reflection, and integrating them into a structured framework, traders can act **resonantly rather than reactively**, gaining foresight and coherence in their market engagement.

"The market whispers its intentions long before it shouts; those who listen to emotional cues move with anticipation rather than hindsight."

12.3 Recognizing Subtle Trend Shifts

Trends in markets rarely start with explosive moves; they often **emerge subtly**, reflecting gradual shifts in collective sentiment, perception, and energy. Recognizing these subtle trend shifts before they become obvious allows traders to **align early with market momentum**, capture opportunities efficiently, and avoid being trapped in lagging reactions.

Nature of Subtle Trend Shifts

- **Gradual Accumulation or Distribution:** - Small, consistent buy or sell activity over time can signal the **beginning of accumulation or distribution**, even when price change appears muted. - Example: A stock quietly moving within a tight range while volume slightly increases can indicate a **latent trend forming**.

- **Micro-Pattern Formation:** - Early trend shifts manifest as **micro-oscillations, subtle higher highs/lower lows, or volume-weighted price changes**. - Detecting these patterns requires **close observation of short-term charts** and order flow.

- **Shift in Emotional Energy:** - Subtle trend changes often coincide with **emotional leading indicators** such as shifting sentiment, changing fear-greed balance, or renewed optimism/pessimism in the market.

Detection Methods

1. **Volume-Price Analysis:** - Observe small increases in volume during minor price moves. - Sustained volume growth with limited price

movement can indicate **preparatory market behavior** for a larger trend.

2. **Divergence Analysis:** - Compare price movement with technical or emotional indicators (e.g., RSI, order flow, sentiment data). - Divergences often signal that a **trend may be forming beneath the surface**.

3. **Order Flow and Depth Observation:** - Track **bid-ask imbalances, hidden orders, and sudden liquidity shifts**. - Changes in the depth of market can reveal the **intent of larger participants**, which often precedes visible trend changes.

4. **Timeframe Alignment:** - Cross-reference **micro-trends on shorter timeframes with broader trends** on longer timeframes. - Subtle shifts often start in one timeframe and propagate outward.

Practical Applications

- Enter positions **early in emerging trends** by observing micro-movements and volume patterns before the trend becomes apparent on standard charts.
- Adjust risk and position sizing **gradually**, in alignment with trend confirmation through multiple indicators.
- Avoid premature reactions to noise by **confirming trend shifts** across emotional, volume, and micro-pattern signals.

Exercises for Traders

- Select a liquid market instrument and **mark small accumulations or distributions** over several days. Compare these observations with subsequent trend developments.
- Track micro-oscillations and bid-ask shifts, noting how **minor repeated patterns anticipate trend initiation**.
- Reflect in a trading journal on instances where you **recognized or missed subtle trend shifts**, and analyze the contributing emotional and energetic signals.

Conclusion

Subtle trend shifts are the **quiet currents beneath visible market waves**. By detecting these early signals through a combination of **volume analysis, micro-pattern recognition, emotional indicators, and order flow observation**, traders can position themselves ahead of larger movements. Mastering the recognition of subtle trend shifts transforms trading from **reactive**

execution to resonant alignment, enhancing both decision quality and timing.

"Trends whisper before they roar; those who hear the whisper move in resonance with the market's hidden energy."

Chapter 13

Market Memory and Echoes

Markets are living systems with a **memory of past events, emotions, and collective behaviors**. Every rally, panic, and correction leaves an imprint on trader psychology and market structure. These imprints influence future price action, shaping expectations, reactions, and sentiment long after the original events have passed.

This chapter examines how **historical emotional cycles, recurring sentiment patterns, and psychological inertia** form the unseen architecture behind market behavior. Understanding these dynamics allows traders to anticipate trends, recognize latent energy in price movements, and align their actions with the market's underlying emotional rhythm rather than reacting purely to surface-level signals.

By exploring market memory and echoes, we aim to provide a **framework for perceiving the subtle continuity of market energy**, linking past events with present opportunities and helping traders make **resonant, informed, and emotionally calibrated decisions**.

13.1 Past Emotional Cycles Influencing Present Behavior

Markets are shaped not only by current events but also by the **emotional residue of past cycles**. Traders collectively remember periods of fear, greed, hope, and panic, and these memories influence present-day behavior, often in subtle yet powerful ways. Understanding these past emotional cycles is essential for anticipating market reactions and aligning trading decisions with underlying sentiment.

Emotional Residue in Market Behavior

- **Trauma and Optimism:** Major market events such as crashes, bubbles, or extended rallies leave psychological marks on traders. Example: Investors who experienced a severe market decline may react cautiously during future rallies, even when fundamentals are strong, resulting in **slower accumulation or muted enthusiasm**.
- **Anchoring to Past Extremes:** Prices associated with historical highs or lows act as **anchors** in trader perception. Collective memory often causes traders to **overemphasize past levels**, influencing buying or selling behavior at these points.
- **Conditioned Responses:** Repetition of specific price behaviors under emotional stress conditions the market's collective psyche. Traders may **anticipate recurring patterns** based on previous experiences, creating a self-reinforcing cycle of expectation and reaction.

Mechanisms of Influence

- **Cognitive Biases:** - *Recency bias* and *availability bias* make recent emotional events disproportionately influential. - Traders often interpret new information through the lens of **past market outcomes**, affecting decision-making.
- **Herd Behavior:** - Shared experiences of past emotional cycles amplify herd behavior. - When a large group of traders collectively recalls previous patterns, their synchronized actions can **recreate similar price movements**, reinforcing the market memory.
- **Sentiment Lag:** - Emotional cycles create inertia, delaying the market's reaction to new information. - Traders influenced by past highs or lows may hesitate, causing **gradual rather than immediate adjustments** in price.

Practical Applications

- Track historical periods of extreme sentiment and observe how **current market reactions mirror past behavior**.
- Maintain a trading journal documenting **emotional cues** and their correlation with subsequent price movements.
- Use awareness of past emotional cycles to **anticipate possible overreactions or underreactions**, positioning trades in alignment with emerging trends rather than reacting impulsively.

Conclusion

Past emotional cycles leave **lasting imprints** on markets. By observing how fear, greed, hope, and panic influence present-day behavior, traders can gain foresight into market tendencies, anticipate latent energy, and align their actions with the market's underlying rhythm. In essence, the market carries a memory of emotion those who learn to read it can trade with **resonance and anticipation rather than reaction**.

"The market does not forget; it whispers the lessons of the past to those who listen."

13.2 Recurring Sentiment Patterns

Market behavior is profoundly influenced by human emotion, and these emotions often **repeat in cyclical patterns**. While no two market events are exactly alike, the collective psychology of traders produces identifiable waves of sentiment that echo across time, creating **predictable rhythms of fear, greed, hope, and despair**.

Nature of Recurring Sentiment Patterns

- **Cyclicality of Emotion:** - Market participants typically move through similar emotional sequences in response to gains, losses, and volatility. - Example: A sustained rally often generates **optimism → excitement → euphoria → complacency**, which is eventually followed by caution, fear, and sometimes panic.
- **Amplitude Variations:** - Emotional waves can vary in intensity depending on market context, liquidity, and external factors. - Large macro events amplify sentiment swings, while micro-movements generate smaller oscillations.
- **Cross-Market Resonance:** - Sentiment patterns often propagate across correlated markets. Fear in equities can spill into commodities or FX, creating **synchronized emotional waves**.

Mechanisms Behind Pattern Recurrence

- **Herd Behavior and Collective Cognition:** - Traders observe and mimic the actions of peers, reinforcing recurrent patterns of emotion. - Shared memory of past market cycles strengthens these repetitions, as participants **expect and act according to familiar sequences**.

- **Cognitive Bias Reinforcement:** - Biases such as overconfidence, loss aversion, and recency effect perpetuate emotional cycles. - For instance, after a period of gains, overconfidence may accelerate greed, while after losses, heightened caution intensifies fear.
- **Feedback Loops:** - Price movements driven by collective sentiment reinforce the underlying emotion. - Example: Rising prices generate optimism, which fuels more buying, creating a **self-reinforcing cycle** until external shocks or exhaustion occur.

Detecting Recurring Sentiment Patterns

- **Sentiment Indices:** Track market surveys, put-call ratios, and social media sentiment to identify **overly bullish or bearish extremes**.
- **Price-Volume Analysis:** Look for **repeating patterns of accumulation, distribution, or consolidation** that correspond with emotional cycles.
- **Historical Pattern Comparison:** Compare current market behavior with previous cycles to **anticipate potential turning points**.

Practical Applications

- Position trades in alignment with **emotional cycle phases**, rather than reacting solely to price action.
- Adjust **risk management strategies** according to the amplitude and stage of the sentiment wave.
- Maintain a **sentiment journal** to record and reflect on observed patterns, helping to refine intuition and anticipatory skills.

Conclusion

Recurring sentiment patterns act as the **underlying rhythm of market behavior**, guiding collective action long before it becomes visible in price. By understanding these cycles, traders can **anticipate market movements, align their actions with the prevailing emotional currents, and avoid being caught off-guard by predictable waves of fear or greed.**

"Emotion is the heartbeat of the market; learning its rhythm allows you to move in resonance rather than resistance."

13.3 Psychological Market Inertia

Markets, like human behavior, often exhibit **resistance to change**, even when presented with new information. This phenomenon, known as psychological market inertia, arises from the combined weight of past experiences, collective sentiment, and cognitive biases. Understanding this inertia allows traders to **anticipate delayed reactions, prolonged trends, and subtle opportunities** that are invisible to those focusing only on immediate price action.

Nature of Market Inertia

- **Emotional Carryover:** - Market participants carry forward emotions from previous cycles, which **delay adaptation** to new developments. - Example: After a market crash, traders may remain cautious during subsequent rallies, slowing the recovery momentum.
- **Cognitive Anchoring:** - Traders often **anchor** their expectations to past price levels, highs, or lows, creating resistance to immediate trend changes. - This anchoring reinforces price plateaus and consolidations, even in the face of supportive fundamentals.
- **Collective Herd Resistance:** - Inertia is amplified by the **synchronized caution of large groups of traders**. - When a majority hesitates to act, trends develop gradually, and reversal signals may take longer to manifest.

Mechanisms Behind Inertia

- **Behavioral Biases:** - Biases such as loss aversion, confirmation bias, and status quo bias make traders reluctant to act contrary to prior expectations. - These biases slow the **market's response to new information**, reinforcing existing trends.
- **Reinforcement of Past Patterns:** - Repeated exposure to familiar price behaviors **conditions trader expectations**, creating psychological inertia that persists even under changing conditions.
- **Delayed Feedback Loops:** - Emotional and cognitive inertia creates **lag in collective reactions**, often resulting in overshooting or undershooting of price movements once the pent-up energy is released.

Implications for Traders

- **Trend Anticipation:** Understanding inertia helps traders **identify latent momentum** that has yet to express fully in price action.

- **Avoiding Premature Reactions:** Traders who recognize inertia can resist the urge to exit or enter prematurely, aligning their decisions with the **actual unfolding of market sentiment**.
- **Enhanced Risk Management:** By accounting for psychological resistance, traders can **adjust position sizing, timing, and stop-loss levels**, mitigating the risk of reacting to transient market noise.

Practical Observations and Exercises

- Track historical examples where price **lagged behind major news or sentiment shifts**, noting the duration and magnitude of inertia.
- Maintain a journal of observed **market hesitations and delayed reactions**, linking them to prior emotional or price cycles.
- Develop a framework for **waiting and observing** before acting, using inertia as a guide to **enter positions at the optimal inflection points**.

Conclusion

Psychological market inertia is the **echo of collective memory** in motion. By recognizing the resistance embedded in trader behavior, one can anticipate delayed reactions, align with emerging trends, and exploit opportunities that arise from the market's slow adaptation. In essence, understanding inertia transforms market observation from reactive speculation into **resonant, anticipatory trading**.

"The market moves not only with news but with the weight of its own history; those who sense its hesitation can act with foresight."

Chapter 14

Cognitive Calibration

Trading is not solely a game of numbers or strategies it is fundamentally a **practice of perception, awareness, and alignment**. The market communicates through subtle signals, emotional undercurrents, and collective energy, and the ability to interpret these cues depends on the trader's **mental, emotional, and perceptual calibration**.

This chapter focuses on developing the internal faculties necessary for **resonant trading**. By aligning mind, emotion, and perception, traders can enhance sensitivity to micro-movements, anticipate market rhythms, and make decisions that are coherent rather than reactionary.

14.1 Aligning Mind, Emotion, and Perception

Trading is as much an **internal discipline** as it is a technical or strategic practice. The most sophisticated strategies fail if the trader's mind, emotions, and perception are not in harmony. Aligning these three faculties mental clarity, emotional balance, and perceptual accuracy is the foundation of **cognitive calibration**, enabling traders to detect subtle signals, interpret market rhythms correctly, and respond with composure.

Mind: Clarity and Focus

- **Objective Thinking:** The mind must process information **without distortion from past experiences or emotional biases**. This includes analyzing charts, news, and patterns while maintaining a clear separation from subjective interpretation.
- **Attention Management:** Traders must cultivate the ability to **focus on relevant signals and filter out distractions**, distinguishing meaningful data from noise.

- **Cognitive Flexibility:** Markets are dynamic and ever-changing. A calibrated mind can **adapt rapidly**, shift perspectives, and avoid rigid attachment to prior assumptions.

Emotion: Balance and Regulation

- **Awareness of Emotional States:** Recognizing fear, greed, impatience, or overconfidence is critical. Awareness allows traders to **prevent emotions from dictating decisions unconsciously**.
- **Regulation Techniques:** Practices such as deep breathing, brief meditation, or mindful pausing before executing trades help **stabilize emotional fluctuations**, maintaining equilibrium even in volatile markets.
- **Emotional Resonance with the Market:** Emotions should not be suppressed but **synchronized with market energy**. Traders can sense subtle shifts in sentiment, aligning their actions with the prevailing emotional currents rather than resisting them.

Perception: Sensitivity and Accuracy

- **Heightened Awareness:** Perception is the lens through which the mind interprets market signals. A calibrated perception **detects micro-movements, subtle volume changes, and shifts in trader sentiment**.
- **Pattern Recognition:** Recognizing recurring emotional and behavioral patterns allows traders to **anticipate market reactions** before they fully manifest in price.
- **Integration with Mind and Emotion:** Accurate perception alone is insufficient; it must be **interpreted through a clear mind and balanced emotion** to produce informed and effective decisions.

Practical Strategies for Alignment

- Begin trading sessions with a **brief mental check-in**, assessing clarity, emotional state, and attentional focus.
- Maintain an **emotional log** during trading to identify patterns of emotional reactivity.
- Practice **observational exercises** to notice subtle market signals without immediate reaction, reinforcing perceptual accuracy.
- Use reflective pauses between trades to **ensure decisions remain aligned across mind, emotion, and perception**.

Conclusion

Aligning mind, emotion, and perception forms the **core of cognitive calibration**. Traders who cultivate this internal harmony are able to **sense the market's emotional undercurrents, filter out noise, and act with precision and confidence**. This alignment transforms trading from a reactive activity into a **resonant, anticipatory practice**, where observation, feeling, and analysis converge to guide effective action.

> *"The market speaks in whispers and echoes; a calibrated mind, balanced emotion, and keen perception are the instruments to hear it clearly."*

14.2 Mindfulness and Journaling Exercises

Mindfulness and journaling are powerful tools for developing **cognitive calibration** in trading. They enhance awareness of internal states, refine perception of market signals, and provide a structured framework to **observe, reflect, and act with clarity**. By cultivating these practices, traders can bridge the gap between emotional experience and rational decision-making, transforming reactive behavior into deliberate, resonant action.

Mindfulness in Trading

Mindfulness involves **present-moment awareness without judgment**, enabling traders to observe thoughts, emotions, and market phenomena clearly. Key aspects include:

- **Focused Attention:** Direct attention to the current market state, noticing price movements, volume shifts, and emotional reactions without distraction or interpretation.
- **Emotional Awareness:** Recognize internal reactions fear, excitement, impatience as **informative signals**, rather than triggers for impulsive action.
- **Breathing and Pausing Techniques:** Use deliberate breathing or short pauses during trading to **reset mental and emotional state**, allowing decisions to arise from calm observation rather than stress or reflex.
- **Non-Attachment:** Accept both gains and losses without letting them dominate mental state. This fosters **equanimity**, reducing the risk of overreacting to short-term market noise.

Journaling for Cognitive Calibration

A structured trading journal provides a **tangible record** of thoughts, emotions, decisions, and outcomes. Key practices include:

- **Pre-Trade Reflections:** Record the current emotional state, market context, rationale for potential trades, and anticipated risks. This prepares the mind to **align perception and intention**.
- **Post-Trade Analysis:** Document what occurred, how emotions influenced decisions, and what signals were observed. Reflect on discrepancies between expectation and outcome to **identify recurring biases or blind spots**.
- **Pattern Tracking:** Over time, journals reveal **patterns in emotional response and market behavior**, highlighting moments of clarity versus reactivity.
- **Self-Assessment Metrics:** Include ratings of focus, emotional balance, and decision alignment after each session. This quantitative feedback helps **measure progress in cognitive calibration**.

Practical Exercises

1. **Daily Mindfulness Session (5–10 minutes):** Sit quietly, observe breath, and notice mental and emotional states. Then visualize upcoming trading sessions, imagining calm, attentive, and aligned decision-making.
2. **Trade Observation Without Action:** For a short period, watch the market without placing trades. Record subtle emotional reactions and market micro-signals, training the mind to **observe without immediate intervention**.
3. **Emotion-Triggered Reflection:** Whenever a strong emotion arises during trading, pause and document: - Emotion experienced - Triggering market event - Immediate impulse - Observed alternative responses
4. **Weekly Synthesis:** Review journal entries weekly to identify recurring **emotional patterns, perceptual blind spots, and moments of aligned decision-making**.

Benefits for Traders

- Enhances **self-awareness**, reducing the influence of unconscious biases.
- Improves **emotional regulation**, allowing for measured and rational decisions.

- Strengthens **pattern recognition**, both in personal behavior and market dynamics.
- Cultivates **anticipatory, resonant trading**, where actions are aligned with both internal state and external market rhythms.

Conclusion

Mindfulness and journaling are not ancillary practices they are central to **cognitive calibration**. They transform trading into a reflective, attentive, and resonant activity, enabling traders to respond to markets with **clarity, composure, and precision** rather than reactionary impulse.

"Awareness is the leverage of the mind; reflection is the path to aligned action."

14.3 Training Awareness for Subtle Signals

Markets constantly communicate through **subtle signals** small price movements, shifts in volume, micro-patterns, and nuanced sentiment cues. These signals often precede larger moves and provide traders with **early insight into market direction and collective behavior**. Training awareness to detect and interpret these signals is a central skill of cognitive calibration, bridging perception, emotion, and action.

Understanding Subtle Market Signals

- **Micro-Price Movements:** - Tiny deviations in price, often unnoticed by casual observers, can indicate **early shifts in supply and demand**. - Example: Minor support or resistance reactions before a major breakout signal underlying market tension.
- **Volume and Order Flow Patterns:** - Changes in trading volume, bid-ask spreads, or order book dynamics reveal **hidden trader intentions** and can precede significant moves.
- **Sentiment Nuances:** - Social sentiment, news tone, and intra-day chatter can produce **micro-emotional fluctuations**, which often manifest first in minor price oscillations.
- **Behavioral Echoes:** - Repeated reactions to recurring patterns such as panic selling near prior lows or hesitant buying at prior highs create **predictable early indicators**.

Mechanisms to Train Awareness

- **Focused Observation:** - Dedicate time to watch the market without placing trades. - Note even small fluctuations and the context in which they occur. This trains the mind to **spot signals before they escalate**.
- **Pattern Recognition Exercises:** - Maintain a log of recurring micro-patterns, including candlestick formations, intraday momentum shifts, and volume anomalies. - Compare across multiple sessions to **internalize the rhythm of subtle market movements**.
- **Emotional Coupling:** - Observe how subtle market cues influence your emotions. - By linking internal reactions to micro-signals, traders **learn to read markets as extensions of collective psychology**.
- **Simulated Micro-Decision Drills:** - Use historical charts or replay platforms to practice **making decisions based solely on early, subtle signals**. - Record outcomes and reflect on accuracy, bias, and reaction time.

Integration with Cognitive Calibration

Awareness of subtle signals is most effective when combined with **mindfulness and journaling**:

- Pre-trade mindfulness ensures clarity to perceive faint cues.
- Journaling reinforces learning by documenting micro-signals, associated emotions, and resulting decisions.
- Repeated practice builds a **mental "signal radar"**, enhancing anticipation and timing for trades.

Practical Exercises

1. **Micro-Movement Observation:** - Select a market and monitor it for short intervals, noting minor price and volume fluctuations and hypothesizing potential consequences.
2. **Signal-to-Emotion Mapping:** - Track your emotional response to subtle market cues to identify biases and improve **perceptual calibration**.
3. **Early-Stage Pattern Journaling:** - Maintain a dedicated log of observed micro-patterns, emerging trends, and outcomes to develop **anticipatory insight**.

Conclusion

Training awareness for subtle signals elevates trading from reactive to **pre-emptive and resonant action**. By perceiving the market's faint cues and understanding their emotional and cognitive context, traders can position themselves ahead of larger moves, aligning their decisions with **the natural rhythm of market behavior** rather than reacting to its aftermath.

"The market whispers long before it shouts; those who listen closely shape the course of their own trades."

Chapter 15

Coherence vs. Noise

In trading, the line between signal and noise is often blurred. Markets are inherently chaotic, influenced by countless participants, events, and emotional undercurrents. The ability to **distinguish coherent, actionable information from reactive noise** is a hallmark of a resonant trader.

This chapter explores the principles of coherence in trading the alignment of mind, emotion, and perception with genuine market signals while contrasting them with reactionary, noise-driven behavior. By understanding and applying these concepts, traders can **filter out distractions, make intentional decisions, and maintain composure amidst volatility**.

15.1 Distinguishing Aligned Decisions from Reactionary Trades

In trading, not all actions are created equal. Some trades arise from **deliberate analysis, emotional balance, and perceptual clarity**, while others are reactionary, impulsive, or driven by unprocessed emotional stimuli. Distinguishing between **aligned decisions** and **reactionary trades** is critical for long-term consistency and mastery.

Aligned Decisions

Aligned decisions emerge from a state where **mind, emotion, and perception are synchronized**. These trades are characterized by:

- **Intentionality:** Actions are guided by a clear rationale, informed by both data and awareness of market sentiment.
- **Emotional Regulation:** The trader's emotional state supports the decision rather than overrides it. Fear, greed, or frustration are acknowledged but do not dominate.

- **Perceptual Accuracy:** Subtle signals, patterns, and market rhythms are recognized and interpreted accurately, providing a clear basis for timing and execution.
- **Consistency:** Aligned trades are repeatable under similar conditions because they are based on **principled frameworks** rather than situational impulses.

Reactionary Trades

Reactionary trades occur when the trader is influenced primarily by **immediate emotions, external noise, or cognitive biases**. Common traits include:

- **Impulsivity:** Decisions are made hastily, often in response to sudden price swings, news events, or peer behavior, without structured analysis.
- **Emotional Dominance:** Fear, greed, or frustration directly drive entry, exit, or sizing decisions, leading to inconsistent outcomes.
- **Overreaction to Noise:** Traders react to **short-term fluctuations or rumors**, mistaking transient volatility for meaningful signals.
- **Lack of Reflection:** Reactionary trades are rarely documented, reviewed, or analyzed for patterns, limiting learning and growth.

Practical Techniques to Promote Aligned Decisions

1. **Pause Before Execution:** Introduce a short deliberate pause before placing any trade to assess whether the decision is grounded or reactive.
2. **Check Internal Alignment:** Ask: "Am I calm? Am I perceiving the market clearly? Are my actions intentional or emotional?" Only proceed when alignment is affirmed.
3. **Document Rationale:** Record the reasoning, signals, and anticipated outcomes for each trade. This habit reinforces **intentional decision-making** and makes patterns of reactionary behavior visible.
4. **Use Predefined Criteria:** Establish rules for entry, exit, and sizing based on aligned frameworks. Reactionary impulses are reduced when **decisions are guided by principles rather than emotions**.

Case Illustration

Consider a market scenario where a sudden price spike occurs:

- A reactionary trader immediately buys, driven by **fear of missing out (FOMO)**, without evaluating context.
- An aligned trader pauses, observes volume, order flow, and sentiment patterns, then decides whether to participate based on **principled assessment and internal calibration**.

The outcome demonstrates how **emotional alignment and clarity** dictate whether a trade becomes a consistent success or a reactive loss.

Conclusion

Aligned decisions are the hallmark of mastery, whereas reactionary trades reflect uncalibrated perception and unmanaged emotion. By **developing awareness, reflective practices, and principled frameworks**, traders can consistently distinguish signal from noise, making choices that are coherent, repeatable, and resonant with the underlying market rhythm.

"Clarity in action comes from harmony within; chaos is the shadow of unaligned choices."

15.2 Filtering Market Chaos

Markets are inherently noisy systems, influenced by countless participants, conflicting information, and emotional undercurrents. Amid this complexity, traders must **identify meaningful signals** while disregarding distractions, rumors, and random fluctuations. Filtering market chaos is essential for **coherent decision-making and sustained trading performance**.

Understanding Market Noise

Market noise refers to **irrelevant or misleading information** that can obscure true signals. Common sources include:

- **Short-term price volatility:** Minute-to-minute swings that may not reflect underlying trends.
- **Excessive news flow:** Headlines, rumors, or analyst opinions that create emotional reactions without strategic value.
- **Social sentiment overreactions:** Amplified reactions on forums or social media that do not align with fundamental or technical patterns.
- **Cognitive bias amplification:** Traders projecting personal fears, hopes, or expectations onto the market.

Techniques to Filter Noise

1. **Define a Signal Framework:** Establish clear criteria for what constitutes a meaningful signal. This may include technical indicators, emotional wave observations, order flow anomalies, or macro-context. Signals outside this framework are treated as noise.

2. **Timeframe Segmentation:** Observe markets across multiple timeframes. Short-term fluctuations often contain more noise, while longer-term trends reveal **coherent patterns**. Align trades with the timeframe most relevant to your strategy.

3. **Emotional Checkpoints:** Pause and assess your emotional state before reacting. Strong emotional responses often indicate that noise is being mistaken for signal.

4. **Filter Inputs:** Limit sources of market information to a curated set of reliable channels. Avoid overconsumption of real-time news, social media chatter, and conflicting analyst opinions.

5. **Pattern Recognition Training:** Practice recognizing **consistent micro-patterns and recurring signals** over time. Repetition helps distinguish true signals from random fluctuations.

Mindset for Navigating Chaos

Filtering market chaos is not only a technical process but also a mental discipline. Key mindset elements include:

- **Patience:** Wait for signals to emerge clearly rather than reacting prematurely.

- **Detachment:** Avoid becoming emotionally attached to specific outcomes or positions.

- **Curiosity:** Observe market behavior objectively, as if conducting an experiment, rather than seeking confirmation of prior beliefs.

- **Flexibility:** Be willing to revise signal definitions as market dynamics evolve, without succumbing to noise-driven indecision.

Practical Exercises

1. **Noise Journaling:** Track moments when emotional reactions were triggered by irrelevant fluctuations. Reflect on the source of the distraction and alternative responses.

2. **Signal Validation Drill:** Record potential signals and monitor outcomes before acting. Only act when a **signal demonstrates reliability** according to your framework.

3. **Information Diet Audit:** Review all sources of market information consumed in a day. Identify which contributed to clarity versus confusion, and adjust input streams accordingly.

Conclusion

Successfully filtering market chaos allows traders to **focus on what truly matters**, acting with alignment rather than reaction. By combining structured signal frameworks, emotional awareness, and disciplined information management, traders can transform the apparent randomness of the market into **coherent, actionable insight**.

"In the midst of market noise, clarity is not the absence of movement but the presence of discernment."

15.3 Maintaining Emotional Stability

Emotional stability is a cornerstone of coherent trading. Markets are dynamic, often volatile, and continuously interacting with our psychological and physiological responses. Without stability, even the most well-analyzed signals can be misinterpreted, and aligned decisions can devolve into reactionary trades. This section explores the principles, strategies, and practical exercises for cultivating emotional resilience in trading.

Understanding Emotional Dynamics in Trading

- **Emotions as Signals:** Emotions are not inherently detrimental; they provide information about your perception of risk, market ambiguity, and personal biases. Recognizing emotions as data allows you to respond constructively rather than reactively.

- **Stress and Market Volatility:** Sudden price swings, unexpected news, or rapid trend reversals can trigger **fight-or-flight responses**, leading to impulsive decisions. Awareness of these triggers is critical to maintain composure.

- **Feedback Loops Between Mind and Market:** Emotional instability can amplify market perception errors, creating self-reinforcing cycles of poor decision-making. Stable traders are better able to **break these loops** and maintain objectivity.

Techniques for Emotional Stability

1. **Mindfulness and Breathing Exercises:** - Incorporate short mindfulness practices before, during, and after trading sessions. - Focused breathing helps regulate physiological arousal and maintain **mental clarity under pressure**.

2. **Predefined Trading Plans:** - Establish clear entry, exit, and risk-management rules in advance. - Predefined plans reduce decision stress by **minimizing impulsive judgment calls** during high volatility.

3. **Emotional Journaling:** - Record emotional states alongside trades, noting triggers and responses. - Over time, this practice develops **self-awareness and predictive insight** into personal reactions.

4. **Pause and Reflection Protocol:** - Before executing any trade, take a deliberate pause to assess both market signals and internal state. - Ask: "Am I responding to the market or to my emotions?" Only act when alignment is confirmed.

5. **Resilience Training:** - Expose yourself to simulated market stress or historical volatility in controlled environments. - Practice remaining calm and executing plans under pressure to **strengthen emotional endurance**.

Maintaining Long-Term Emotional Equilibrium

- **Rest and Recovery:** Sufficient sleep, exercise, and breaks from trading prevent cumulative stress that undermines decision-making.

- **Perspective and Detachment:** View individual trades as part of a broader journey. Avoid over-identifying with wins or losses.

- **Support Systems:** Mentors, peer traders, or trading communities can provide guidance, reflection, and emotional validation, reducing isolation-induced stress.

Practical Exercises

1. **Daily Emotional Check-In:** - Rate your emotional state before and after trading sessions. - Note triggers and patterns to build self-awareness.

2. **Controlled Stress Drills:** - Simulate rapid market changes in practice environments and practice executing trades calmly under pressure.

3. **Post-Trade Reflection:** - Document decisions, emotional reactions, and deviations from plan. - Analyze patterns to identify emotional vulnerabilities and reinforce stability.

Conclusion

Emotional stability transforms trading from a reactive struggle into a **resonant practice of observation, anticipation, and aligned action**. By developing self-awareness, structured protocols, and resilience, traders can navigate the unpredictable market landscape with composure, consistency, and confidence.

"Stable emotions are the vessel through which clarity flows; without them, even insight drifts into chaos."

Chapter 16

Resonant Decision-Making Framework

Trading is not merely a mechanical exercise of indicators and strategies it is an **interactive process of perception, emotion, and deliberate action**. Markets are living systems, resonating with collective human behavior, and successful traders must navigate both the external environment and their internal states.

The Resonant Decision-Making Framework provides a **structured, holistic approach** to trading that integrates observation, emotional awareness, analysis, alignment, and execution. It is designed to transform raw market data and internal signals into coherent, intentional decisions that are in harmony with both market rhythms and personal mental calibration.

16.1 Observe → Feel → Analyze → Align → Act

The Resonant Decision-Making Framework is a holistic approach to trading that integrates **perception, emotion, analysis, alignment, and execution** into a coherent, repeatable workflow. Each step builds upon the previous, ensuring that decisions are both **informed and emotionally grounded**, minimizing reactionary behavior while maximizing resonance with market rhythms.

Step 1: Observe

Observation is the foundation of all effective trading. It involves **attentive, unbiased perception** of market conditions, data, and micro-signals.

- **Market Observation:** Track price movements, volume, order flow, and sentiment without immediate judgment.

- **Context Awareness:** Situate observations within macro trends, historical cycles, and broader economic or geopolitical factors.
- **Self-Observation:** Monitor your own mental and emotional state, noting biases, stress, or anticipatory impulses that may distort perception.

Step 2: Feel

Feeling emphasizes **emotional attunement**. Markets are collective emotional systems, and sensing the undercurrents can provide early, subtle signals.

- **Emotional Resonance:** Identify your own emotional response to observed patterns fear, excitement, hesitation and differentiate it from the market's emotional signals.
- **Empathy with Market Sentiment:** Sense prevailing moods such as greed, panic, or indecision among market participants.
- **Calibration Exercises:** Techniques such as breathing, brief meditation, or micro-pauses can enhance emotional clarity.

Step 3: Analyze

Analysis translates observation and emotional sensing into **structured insight**.

- **Data Synthesis:** Combine technical indicators, market memory, and sentiment signals to form a coherent understanding.
- **Pattern Recognition:** Identify recurring structures, micro-oscillations, and potential turning points.
- **Risk Assessment:** Evaluate probabilities, position sizing, and potential outcomes without emotional interference.
- **Avoiding Over-Analysis:** Balance detail with timeliness; analysis is a tool to inform action, not to paralyze it.

Step 4: Align

Alignment ensures that your **internal state, objectives, and market insight** are synchronized before action.

- **Internal Checkpoint:** Confirm that emotions, intuition, and rationale support the same decision.
- **Intentionality:** Ensure that every action is purposeful, not impulsive.

- **Flow Alignment:** Actions should resonate with market rhythm; entering too early or too late can disrupt alignment.
- **Mental Calibration:** Use reflection or brief journaling to solidify clarity and confidence.

Step 5: Act

Action is the culmination of observation, feeling, analysis, and alignment.

- **Decisive Execution:** Enter, adjust, or exit positions based on the integrated insights.
- **Mindful Engagement:** Maintain emotional awareness during execution, observing outcomes without attachment.
- **Feedback Loop:** Record results and emotional states for later reflection, strengthening the framework over time.

Practical Example

Consider a trader monitoring a volatile asset:

1. **Observe:** The trader notices unusual volume and subtle shifts in market depth.
2. **Feel:** A sense of cautious optimism emerges, indicating collective buying pressure.
3. **Analyze:** Patterns suggest a potential breakout; risk/reward ratios are calculated.
4. **Align:** Emotional state is calm, reasoning and intuition concur, and timing aligns with expected market rhythm.
5. **Act:** The trader enters a position, monitors signals, and records observations for future reflection.

Benefits of the Framework

- Reduces impulsive, reactionary trades.
- Enhances clarity in high-volatility situations.
- Creates a **repeatable, resonant workflow** that integrates emotional and cognitive insight.
- Builds long-term trading mastery by linking awareness to action.

Conclusion

The Observe → Feel → Analyze → Align → Act framework transforms trading from reactive behavior into a **deliberate, resonant practice**. By following this process consistently, traders can harmonize with market rhythms, interpret subtle signals accurately, and execute decisions with confidence and clarity.

"Action without awareness is noise; alignment turns observation into resonance."

16.2 Applying the Framework Across Timeframes

The Resonant Decision-Making Framework Observe → Feel → Analyze → Align → Act is **highly versatile** and can be applied across multiple trading timeframes, from intraday scalping to long-term position trading. Adapting the framework for different horizons ensures that traders maintain **coherence, emotional alignment, and strategic clarity** regardless of market context.

Understanding Timeframe Dynamics

Each trading timeframe presents unique challenges:

- **Intraday/Short-Term:** Fast-moving markets, high volatility, and frequent noise. Requires rapid observation, quick emotional calibration, and precise execution.
- **Swing/Medium-Term:** Trends unfold over days to weeks. Emotional influence is less acute than intraday, but patience and timing are critical to avoid premature actions.
- **Long-Term/Position Trading:** Market cycles, macro factors, and recurring sentiment patterns dominate. Observation is broader, emotions are more stable, and alignment involves strategic goals and risk management over extended periods.

Step Adaptations Across Timeframes

1. **Observe:**
    - Short-term: Monitor order flow, micro-volatility, and real-time sentiment changes.

- Medium-term: Focus on emerging trends, volume patterns, and market memory effects.
- Long-term: Track macroeconomic signals, structural market shifts, and recurring emotional cycles.

2. **Feel:**
   - Short-term: Recognize immediate emotional reactions and micro-resonance with market swings.
   - Medium-term: Sense the momentum of broader trends and collective market psychology.
   - Long-term: Align personal objectives and intuition with cyclical market energy and collective investor sentiment.

3. **Analyze:**
   - Short-term: Rapid technical analysis, tick charts, and micro-pattern recognition.
   - Medium-term: Combine technical indicators with sentiment mapping and market memory observations.
   - Long-term: Macro-level analysis, fundamental evaluation, and identification of recurring market cycles.

4. **Align:**
   - Short-term: Instantaneous emotional regulation, confirmation of intuition, and risk alignment.
   - Medium-term: Patience and alignment with trend, ensuring positions match risk/reward expectations.
   - Long-term: Strategic coherence with overarching portfolio objectives, risk tolerance, and life goals.

5. **Act:**
   - Short-term: Rapid entries/exits with micro-position sizing.
   - Medium-term: Adjust positions in response to trend confirmations and sentiment shifts.
   - Long-term: Execute portfolio-level decisions with a focus on cumulative resonance rather than immediate outcome.

Timeframe Integration

Traders often operate across multiple timeframes simultaneously. Integration strategies include:

- **Top-Down Alignment:** Begin with long-term observation to set strategic context, then refine decisions at medium and short-term levels.

- **Cross-Timeframe Calibration:** Emotional and analytical signals should be consistent across timeframes; conflicting signals require reassessment.
- **Adaptive Execution:** Scale actions according to timeframe significance small adjustments in short-term trades, larger adjustments in medium-term swing positions, and strategic rebalancing for long-term holdings.

Practical Example

A trader observes a long-term uptrend in a major index:

1. **Long-Term:** The trader aligns portfolio allocation with the macro trend, noting recurring market cycles.
2. **Medium-Term:** Identifies swing corrections and prepares for optimal entry points.
3. **Short-Term:** Executes trades during micro-reversals, using emotional calibration to avoid overreacting to intraday noise.

By integrating all three timeframes, the trader **resonates with market rhythm**, balances risk across horizons, and leverages subtle signals for optimized execution.

Conclusion

Applying the Resonant Decision-Making Framework across timeframes allows traders to **maintain alignment and coherence** at all levels of market engagement. By understanding how observation, emotion, analysis, and action interact differently across intraday, medium-term, and long-term horizons, traders can **enhance precision, reduce noise-driven errors, and create a harmonized approach** that scales with market complexity.

"Time is both a lens and a lever; applying resonance across horizons transforms observation into mastery."

16.3 Reflective Practice for Continuous Improvement

Continuous improvement is a hallmark of mastery in trading. While technical skills, market knowledge, and emotional regulation are essential, sustained growth depends on **systematic reflection and iterative learning**. Reflective practice transforms experience into insight, enabling traders to refine their perception, decision-making, and emotional alignment over time.

The Role of Reflection in Trading

- **Observation Becomes Insight:** By reviewing trades, market conditions, and emotional responses, traders convert raw experience into structured understanding.
- **Pattern Recognition and Memory:** Reflection helps identify recurring emotional and behavioral patterns, enhancing anticipation of future market dynamics.
- **Calibration of Internal State:** Continuous review strengthens emotional self-regulation, reducing reactionary responses to volatility.

Components of Reflective Practice

1. **Trade Journaling:** Maintain a detailed log including:
    - Observations and market conditions
    - Emotional state and cognitive biases
    - Analysis, reasoning, and alignment with strategy
    - Decisions and outcomes

    Over time, patterns in thought, emotion, and execution reveal areas for improvement.
2. **Post-Trade Reflection Sessions:** Conduct brief sessions after each trading day or week to review:
    - Which trades aligned with framework principles?
    - Where emotional reactions deviated from observation-based decisions?
    - How could alignment and timing be improved?
3. **Emotional and Cognitive Debriefing:** Examine emotional triggers and cognitive biases that influenced trades. Identify recurring stressors or impulsive behaviors and implement corrective practices, such as breathing exercises or pause protocols.
4. **Scenario Simulation:** Revisit historical trades or hypothetical market scenarios. Apply the Observe $\rightarrow$ Feel $\rightarrow$ Analyze $\rightarrow$ Align $\rightarrow$ Act framework to explore alternative outcomes and refine decision-making strategies.
5. **Progress Metrics:** Develop metrics to track improvement:
    - Reduction in reactionary trades
    - Improved emotional stability scores
    - Accuracy in recognizing early market signals
    - Consistency of alignment across timeframes

Iterative Learning Process

Reflective practice follows an iterative cycle:

1. **Execute:** Engage with the market using the Resonant Decision-Making Framework.
2. **Record:** Capture observations, emotions, analysis, alignment, and actions in a journal.
3. **Review:** Assess successes, misalignments, and missed opportunities.
4. **Refine:** Adjust mental models, risk management, and alignment strategies.
5. **Repeat:** Apply the refined approach in subsequent trades, creating a feedback loop that continuously improves resonance with market rhythms.

Benefits of Reflective Practice

- Strengthens emotional and cognitive awareness.
- Enhances pattern recognition and anticipation of market behavior.
- Increases consistency and coherence in decision-making.
- Cultivates long-term mastery by transforming experience into actionable insight.
- Builds resilience against unexpected market events by integrating past lessons.

Practical Exercises

1. **Daily Reflection:** Spend 10–15 minutes each evening reviewing trades, emotional responses, and alignment with framework steps.
2. **Weekly Debrief:** Summarize trends, recurring challenges, and improvements in your journal.
3. **Monthly Pattern Analysis:** Identify cycles of behavior and market reactions, and update trading strategies accordingly.
4. **Simulation Practice:** Test refined strategies in a controlled environment to reinforce learning.

Conclusion

Reflective practice is the bridge between **experience and mastery**. By consistently observing, evaluating, and refining your trading approach, you develop a deep understanding of market rhythms, emotional dynamics, and personal cognitive patterns. Over time, this iterative process transforms trading from a reactive activity into a **resonant, intentional, and evolving practice**.

"The market mirrors not only opportunity, but your own patterns. Reflection turns these mirrors into guides."

Part III

Systems of Resonant Trading

Chapter 17

Designing a Resonant Trading System

Markets are not merely mechanical systems of price and volume they are **living, resonant environments**, shaped by collective emotion, cognitive patterns, and behavioral feedback loops. Designing a trading system that thrives in such an environment requires more than indicators or algorithms; it demands **alignment with the rhythms of the market**, integration of intuition with data, and conscious management of emotional energy.

This chapter introduces the concept of a **Resonant Trading System**, a framework that blends principles of flow, energy dynamics, and feedback mechanisms into a coherent approach for market engagement. Unlike traditional systems that focus solely on technical precision or statistical edge, a resonant system prioritizes **psychological, emotional, and perceptual coherence**, allowing traders to operate in harmony with market dynamics.

17.1 Principles: Flow, Energy, Feedback Loops

Designing a resonant trading system begins with understanding the **underlying principles** that govern market behavior and trader interaction. These principles flow, energy, and feedback loops serve as the foundation for aligning strategy, perception, and execution.

Flow: Harmonizing with Market Rhythm

Flow refers to the **state of seamless interaction** between a trader and the market, where observation, analysis, and action occur without friction or hesitation. In trading, flow manifests when a trader can:

- Recognize emerging opportunities intuitively while supported by analytical data.

- Execute trades without emotional resistance or impulsive reaction.
- Maintain awareness of market context while focusing on the present moment.

Achieving flow requires both **mental and emotional calibration**, where the trader is attuned to micro and macro market oscillations. Flow is not merely a psychological state; it is the manifestation of alignment between perception and action within a dynamic market environment.

Energy: Price as Emotional and Cognitive Force

Every market movement is underpinned by **energy**, the aggregated emotional and cognitive activity of market participants. Understanding energy in trading involves:

- **Emotional Energy:** Collective fear, greed, hope, or despair that drives momentum and volatility.
- **Cognitive Energy:** The mental engagement of traders processing information, forming narratives, and making decisions.
- **Energy Transfer:** Price moves can be viewed as **transfers of energy**, where shifts in sentiment propagate through the market like waves.

A resonant system is sensitive to these energy flows, allowing traders to **anticipate shifts** and align their decisions with the natural momentum of the market rather than resist it.

Feedback Loops: Amplification and Attenuation

Markets are highly **interactive systems**, where trader actions influence market movements, which in turn affect trader behavior. These interactions form **feedback loops**, which can be either constructive or destructive:

- **Constructive Loops:** Positive reinforcement occurs when aligned trades amplify favorable market trends, creating a self-reinforcing cycle of insight and action.
- **Destructive Loops:** Misaligned or reactive trades amplify noise, increase volatility, and lead to cascading errors or overreaction.

Recognizing and leveraging feedback loops allows traders to **harness market energy** efficiently. By consciously designing actions to reinforce positive resonance and minimize destructive amplification, traders can maintain coherence and achieve sustainable performance.

Integrating the Principles

The true power of these principles emerges when they are **interconnected**:

- Flow enables **intuitive engagement** with market energy.
- Awareness of energy guides decisions that align with **emerging market trends**.
- Feedback loops provide **real-time calibration**, confirming when the trader is in resonance or when adjustments are required.

Practical Application

To apply these principles:

1. Start by observing micro-movements in price to identify energy buildup.
2. Align attention and emotional state with the current rhythm of the market.
3. Take action that resonates with the market trend, monitoring feedback to adjust execution dynamically.
4. Record outcomes and patterns to refine understanding of flow, energy, and loop interactions.

Conclusion

Understanding and applying **flow, energy, and feedback loops** transforms trading from mechanical execution into a **resonant practice**. Traders who integrate these principles develop systems that are adaptive, responsive, and aligned with both market dynamics and their internal decision-making coherence.

"Trade not against the market, but in harmony with its invisible currents, and resonance becomes your guide."

17.2 Integrating Intuition with Data

A truly resonant trading system combines **objective data analysis** with **subjective intuition**, enabling traders to navigate markets that are both complex and emotionally charged. While data provides measurable insight into market structure, trends, and volatility, intuition allows for **rapid pattern recognition, anticipation of subtle shifts, and alignment with market energy**. Integration of these two dimensions creates a coherent decision-making process that leverages both analytical rigor and perceptual sensitivity.

The Role of Intuition in Trading

Intuition is the ability to recognize patterns, relationships, and opportunities **without conscious analytical processing**. In trading, intuition manifests as:

- Recognizing subtle emotional cues and micro-signals in price action.
- Anticipating potential market reactions before they become visible in standard indicators.
- Sensing the flow and rhythm of market movements, allowing preemptive alignment with trends.

Developing intuition requires experience, reflection, and awareness of both **internal cognitive states** and **external market dynamics**.

The Role of Data in Trading

Data provides the **quantitative foundation** for decision-making, including:

- Price history, volume, order flow, and volatility metrics.
- Technical indicators, trend lines, and statistical signals.
- Economic and macro indicators influencing market sentiment.

Data ensures that intuitive insights are **grounded in reality**, preventing purely emotional or biased decisions.

Combining Intuition and Data

Integration occurs when intuitive perception is **validated, calibrated, or refined** by data:

1. **Observation Phase:** Begin by sensing market flow, emotional energy, and micro-signals intuitively.
2. **Analytical Confirmation:** Check intuitive observations against data price patterns, volume spikes, and sentiment metrics.
3. **Decision Alignment:** Allow data to refine timing, position sizing, and risk management, while intuition guides whether the trade aligns with the overall market rhythm.
4. **Feedback Loop:** Post-trade reflection compares intuitive expectations with actual outcomes, enhancing pattern recognition and predictive accuracy.

Developing Intuition in a Data-Rich Environment

To cultivate intuition while using data:

- Practice **pattern recognition** beyond charts notice emotional micro-movements and market microstructure.
- Maintain a **trading journal** to log intuitive feelings alongside quantitative observations.
- Use data as a **calibration tool**, not a crutch avoid overreliance on indicators that may ignore subtle emotional or perceptual cues.
- Engage in **simulated scenarios** to test intuitive responses against historical or hypothetical market conditions.

Practical Example

A trader senses a subtle shift in market sentiment buyers hesitating despite a bullish trend. Intuition signals caution. Checking the data:

- Volume is slightly declining.
- Volatility is rising in minor price swings.
- Technical indicators are near resistance.

Integration of intuition with these data points leads to a **conscious decision to reduce position size and monitor for confirmation**, instead of reacting impulsively. The trade maintains alignment with market flow while mitigating risk.

Benefits of Integration

- Enhances the ability to anticipate market shifts before they appear in standard indicators.
- Improves consistency by aligning emotional perception with objective reality.
- Strengthens feedback loops through reflective calibration of intuitive insights.
- Fosters long-term mastery by balancing analytical rigor with perceptual sensitivity.

Conclusion

Integrating intuition with data transforms trading from a purely reactive process into a **resonant, anticipatory practice**. Traders who balance perceptual insight with analytical evidence achieve higher alignment with market rhythms, better risk management, and improved decision-making consistency.

"Let data guide your hands, but intuition steer your awareness; in this harmony lies mastery."

17.3 Emotional Alignment Metrics

A resonant trading system is not complete without **monitoring and managing the trader's emotional state**. Emotional alignment metrics provide a structured way to measure, calibrate, and optimize internal states, ensuring that decisions remain coherent with market rhythms. These metrics bridge the gap between **psychological awareness** and **practical trading execution**, transforming subjective experience into actionable insight.

Why Emotional Alignment Matters

Emotions are powerful drivers in market behavior, influencing:

- **Perception of risk and opportunity:** Fear can lead to premature exits, while greed may cause overexposure.
- **Decision-making consistency:** Misaligned emotional states increase reactionary trades and reduce clarity.
- **Pattern recognition and intuition:** Calm, focused awareness enhances the ability to detect subtle signals and anticipate market shifts.

Without alignment, even technically sound strategies can fail due to **emotional interference**.

Core Emotional Alignment Metrics

1. **Emotional State Awareness:** Track mood, stress levels, confidence, and focus before, during, and after trading. Journals or digital tracking tools can quantify these states on a scale (e.g., 1–10) for longitudinal analysis.
2. **Reaction Time Consistency:** Measure the time taken to make decisions in response to market movements. Significant deviation from baseline may indicate emotional disruption.

3. **Decision Confidence Index:** Evaluate confidence in each trade on a scale (e.g., low, medium, high) and compare against outcomes. This metric highlights overconfidence or hesitation patterns.

4. **Alignment Score:** Rate the congruence between intuition, analytical data, and emotional state on each trade. Higher alignment scores correlate with better execution and reduced regret.

5. **Stress-to-Flow Ratio:** Monitor the balance between stress-induced reactions and flow-based actions. High stress-to-flow ratios indicate misalignment, signaling the need for pause, mindfulness, or recalibration.

Tools and Techniques for Measuring Alignment

- **Trading Journals:** Record both external market conditions and internal emotional states, allowing pattern recognition over time.

- **Mindfulness and Meditation Apps:** Track heart rate variability, focus, and calmness during trading sessions.

- **Reflective Checklists:** Quick pre- and post-trade surveys assessing emotional readiness and alignment with strategy.

- **Biofeedback Devices:** Optional tools for measuring physiological responses such as stress levels, which can indicate emotional drift from optimal alignment.

Practical Application

1. **Pre-Trade Calibration:** Before entering a trade, evaluate emotional state, alignment with strategy, and readiness to engage with market flow.

2. **In-Trade Monitoring:** During active trading, observe deviations in emotional or cognitive state and adjust exposure or pause trading if misalignment occurs.

3. **Post-Trade Reflection:** Review trades in light of alignment metrics, identify recurring misalignments, and adjust mental and emotional preparation routines.

Benefits of Emotional Alignment Metrics

- Enhances consistency and coherence in decision-making.

- Reduces impulsive or reactionary trades caused by emotional fluctuations.

- Strengthens resonance with market energy and flow.
- Provides a measurable framework for continuous self-improvement.

Conclusion

Emotional alignment metrics are a **critical bridge** between inner psychological states and external market actions. By systematically tracking, measuring, and calibrating emotional energy, traders ensure that their actions are **not only technically sound but also aligned with both market rhythms and internal coherence**. Mastery of these metrics transforms trading from reactionary behavior into a deliberate, resonant practice.

"The market responds not just to strategy, but to the resonance of the mind that engages it."

Chapter 18

Risk as Energy Modulation

Risk is traditionally viewed as a numerical or statistical concept in trading probability of loss, volatility, or drawdown. While these measures are important, they capture only one dimension of market engagement. In a **resonant trading system**, risk is more than numbers it is a reflection of **emotional energy, cognitive state, and alignment with market rhythms**. Understanding risk as energy allows traders to **modulate exposure in harmony with both external market forces and internal psychological states**.

This chapter introduces the concept of **Risk as Energy Modulation**, emphasizing that position sizing, trade scaling, and mental preparation are all mechanisms to manage the flow of energy through the trader-market interaction. By treating risk as a dynamic, resonant property rather than a static statistic, traders can respond adaptively to market shifts while maintaining coherence and flow.

18.1 Position Sizing as Emotional Frequency Management

Position sizing is one of the most powerful tools in trading, not just for managing financial risk, but also for **modulating emotional and cognitive energy**. Each trade carries an emotional signature fear, hope, excitement, or anxiety which interacts with the market's own energy. By adjusting position size, a trader can **align emotional frequency with market conditions**, maintaining coherence, focus, and flow.

The Emotional Dimension of Position Size

Traditional trading focuses on position sizing purely from a risk-reward perspective, e.g., allocating a fixed percentage of capital based on stop-loss distance or volatility. While important, this approach overlooks the **psychological impact of trade size**:

- **Overexposure:** Large positions amplify emotional intensity, increasing stress, impulsivity, and the likelihood of reactionary decisions.
- **Underexposure:** Very small positions may limit emotional engagement, reducing alertness, intuition, and the ability to sense market flow.
- **Resonant Positioning:** Appropriate sizing creates a balance where emotional energy matches market energy, allowing observation, analysis, and execution without being overwhelmed.

Aligning Position Size with Internal State

Before placing a trade, consider the following:

1. **Assess Emotional Readiness:** Rate your stress, focus, and confidence. High stress may call for reduced exposure, while calm alignment may allow fuller participation.
2. **Evaluate Market Energy:** Determine the intensity and volatility of the market. Highly energetic or chaotic markets may require smaller, controlled positions.
3. **Calibrate to Flow:** Choose a position size that allows engagement with the market rhythm without forcing action or creating excessive emotional strain.

Dynamic Sizing Techniques

Position sizing should be **adaptive**, reflecting both internal and external conditions:

- **Percentage of Risk Capital:** Adjust the percentage based on emotional alignment rather than static rules.
- **Incremental Exposure:** Start with smaller positions and scale up as alignment with flow and confidence increases.
- **Energy Budgeting:** Treat emotional energy as a finite resource; allocate it to trades where resonance is highest.

Practical Example

Imagine a trader considering a position in a volatile market:

- Emotional state: calm but alert.
- Market energy: high volatility but clear directional movement.
- Adaptive position sizing: enter with 50% of typical exposure to maintain alignment, observe resonance, then scale to 100% if emotional and market energies remain coherent.

This approach **prevents overreaction**, reduces regret, and maximizes engagement with market flow.

Feedback and Continuous Calibration

Keep a **position sizing journal** to track emotional responses to trade size:

- Record emotional intensity before, during, and after trades.
- Note deviations from intended position size and outcomes.
- Adjust future sizing based on patterns of emotional coherence or disruption.

Conclusion

Position sizing is more than a risk management tool it is a mechanism for **emotional and energetic alignment**. Traders who calibrate size according to both internal state and market conditions maintain flow, reduce impulsivity, and enhance consistent execution. By treating position sizing as **emotional frequency management**, risk becomes not just a numerical concept but a dynamic, resonant practice.

"The size of your position is the volume of your emotional engagement; align it with the market, and your trades will resonate."

18.2 Scaling In and Out Based on Resonance

Scaling in and out of trades is a critical strategy in a resonant trading system. Rather than committing fully at a single point, traders can **modulate exposure dynamically**, responding to both market energy and their own emotional alignment. This approach allows for **flexibility, risk management, and enhanced synchronization with market flow**.

The Concept of Resonant Scaling

In a resonant trading framework, each position is treated as an energetic interaction between the trader and the market. Scaling in and out allows traders to:

- **Enter gradually:** Avoid emotional overwhelm and confirm market direction before committing full capital.
- **Adjust exposure dynamically:** Increase or decrease position size based on ongoing resonance with market rhythm.
- **Manage uncertainty:** Reduce risk when alignment falters, and capitalize when emotional and market energies converge.

Scaling In: Gradual Engagement

1. **Start Small:** Begin with a fraction of the intended position to gauge market reaction and personal emotional alignment.
2. **Observe Resonance:** Monitor whether price movement, volume, and sentiment reflect expected patterns.
3. **Increase Exposure:** Gradually add to the position as confidence grows and alignment with market flow strengthens.

Example: A trader enters a trending market with 30% of intended exposure. As the trend confirms direction and emotional state remains coherent, additional portions are added in steps of 20–30%, maintaining flow and minimizing reactive stress.

Scaling Out: Controlled Exit

Scaling out is equally important to **capture gains while managing emotional risk**:

- Reduce positions gradually as the market reaches key resistance levels or as emotional intensity increases.
- Avoid abrupt exits that may create regret or overreaction.
- Adjust scaling based on both market energy and internal emotional feedback, maintaining coherence until complete exit.

Example: During a volatile uptrend, a trader begins scaling out at 70% of the expected move. This allows participation in further upside while preventing overexposure when market energy shifts or personal stress rises.

Indicators of Resonance for Scaling

Scaling decisions should be guided by a combination of **market signals** and **internal awareness**:

- **Market Flow:** Continuity of trend, volume consistency, and absence of sudden shocks.
- **Emotional Alignment:** Calm, focused observation and absence of anxiety or overconfidence.
- **Feedback Loops:** Price action confirming or amplifying expected patterns, validating resonance with the trader's perception.

Benefits of Resonant Scaling

- Reduces emotional strain by matching exposure to internal state.
- Enhances adaptability to changing market conditions.
- Allows for learning and feedback at lower risk.
- Maintains alignment with flow, minimizing forced or reactionary actions.

Practical Tips for Implementation

1. Predefine scaling increments and conditions for each trade.
2. Use both technical and intuitive signals to decide when to add or reduce exposure.
3. Maintain a trading journal documenting **emotional resonance and scaling decisions** to refine future trades.
4. Avoid rigid adherence to scale plans if resonance or emotional alignment is compromised; flexibility is key.

Conclusion

Scaling in and out based on resonance transforms trading from a binary action into a **fluid, adaptive practice**. By modulating exposure according to both market energy and emotional alignment, traders can optimize performance, reduce psychological stress, and sustain coherence in both winning and losing scenarios.

> *"Trade not at a fixed point, but in harmony with the pulse of the market and the cadence of your mind."*

18.3 Risk-Adaptive Mental Models

Risk in trading is rarely static; it fluctuates with market conditions, volatility, and the trader's own emotional and cognitive state. Traditional risk frameworks often rely purely on numerical measures stop-losses, leverage limits, or position sizing. While necessary, these methods overlook the **dynamic interaction between psychological state and market energy**. Risk-adaptive mental models bridge this gap by providing **flexible cognitive frameworks** to adjust strategy, position, and behavior in real time.

The Concept of Risk-Adaptive Mental Models

Risk-adaptive mental models are structured approaches to **thinking about risk as a dynamic, energetic system** rather than a fixed number. They help traders:

- Recognize when internal states may amplify perceived risk.
- Adjust exposure based on ongoing assessment of market energy.
- Maintain alignment between intuition, analysis, and emotional state.
- Respond fluidly to uncertainty without overreacting or freezing.

Core Principles

1. **Relative Risk Awareness:** Evaluate risk in relation to both capital and emotional bandwidth. For example, a small financial exposure may still be psychologically overwhelming if emotional alignment is low.
2. **Energy-Based Risk Assessment:** Assess market and internal energy simultaneously. High market volatility combined with high personal stress signals a need to **reduce exposure or pause trading**.
3. **Scenario-Based Thinking:** Consider multiple outcomes, both probable and extreme, before entering a trade. Mentally rehearse responses to each scenario to prevent reactive behavior under pressure.
4. **Adaptive Stop and Scale Rules:** Rather than rigid stop-losses, adjust limits and scaling dynamically based on market energy and emotional state.
5. **Feedback Integration:** Continuously incorporate lessons from past trades, including emotional and behavioral responses, into risk assessment for future trades.

Practical Models for Traders

- **Emotional-Capital Matrix:** Map position size against emotional intensity to identify optimal exposure zones. Avoid trades in high-intensity zones unless flow alignment is strong.
- **Market Resonance Gauge:** Rate market energy and coherence, adjusting position and strategy based on resonance with personal readiness.
- **Scenario Tree Analysis:** Visualize potential market moves and emotional responses, preparing adaptive strategies for each branch of outcomes.
- **Flow-Risk Index:** Combine market volatility, personal emotional state, and confidence to produce a dynamic index guiding risk modulation in real time.

Implementing Risk-Adaptive Thinking

1. Pre-trade: Assess internal alignment and market energy. Define dynamic risk parameters rather than rigid limits.
2. In-trade: Monitor market and emotional signals, scaling exposure and adjusting strategy in real time.
3. Post-trade: Reflect on alignment, deviations from planned risk, and lessons learned to refine future models.

Benefits

- Reduces impulsive reactions and emotional overextension.
- Enhances ability to adapt to changing market conditions.
- Aligns internal energy with external market energy, improving consistency and performance.
- Provides a systematic approach to decision-making under uncertainty.

Conclusion

Risk-adaptive mental models transform risk management from a static, rule-based system into a **dynamic, resonant practice**. By integrating emotional, cognitive, and market signals, traders can modulate exposure, maintain coherence, and navigate uncertainty with confidence. This approach turns risk from a source of anxiety into a **tool for alignment, flow, and strategic advantage**.

"Master risk not by rules alone, but by tuning your mind and energy to the rhythm of the market."

Chapter 19

Flow-Based Execution

Execution is the bridge between observation, analysis, and results. In traditional trading, emphasis is often placed on strategies, indicators, or timing, while the **mental and energetic state of execution** is overlooked. Flow-based execution emphasizes **alignment of mind, emotion, and market rhythm** to act decisively and effectively without force or hesitation.

This chapter introduces the concept of **Flow-Based Execution**, where trades are not just mechanical actions but **resonant interactions with the market**. Peak performance arises when traders recognize and enter moments of market resonance, avoid forced or reactive actions, and cultivate patience and discipline. Execution becomes an art of **synchronization, observation, and aligned action**, rather than mere reaction to charts or signals.

19.1 Identifying Peak Resonance Moments

Peak resonance moments are instances when **market conditions, price movement, and trader state align perfectly**, creating a window for optimal execution. These moments are not dictated solely by technical indicators or signals they emerge from the **interplay of market energy, trader perception, and emotional coherence**. Recognizing these moments allows traders to act decisively while minimizing emotional friction and uncertainty.

The Nature of Resonance

Resonance is a concept borrowed from physics, where systems vibrate most efficiently when their frequency aligns with an external stimulus. In trading, resonance occurs when:

- The trader's attention, emotional state, and focus are fully aligned.
- Market signals, volume, and momentum converge in a coherent pattern.

- Risk and position size match the trader's internal readiness.

During these moments, execution becomes effortless, decisions feel natural, and the probability of favorable outcomes increases not because of luck, but due to **synchronized observation and action**.

Identifying Resonant Conditions

Several factors signal a peak resonance moment:

1. **Market Rhythm:** Look for consistent price patterns, steady trends, or consolidation breakouts that indicate energy buildup.
2. **Volume Alignment:** High resonance is often accompanied by volume that confirms the intended direction of movement.
3. **Emotional Coherence:** Check internal state calm focus, clear judgment, and absence of fear or overexcitement indicate readiness.
4. **Confirmation Across Timeframes:** Multiple timeframes showing alignment strengthen the resonance signal.
5. **Feedback Loops:** Small early movements in the market confirming your observation can indicate a resonant opportunity for scaling in.

Practical Techniques for Recognition

- **Micro-Observation:** Monitor subtle market signals such as momentum shifts, order flow anomalies, or changes in volatility.
- **Journaling and Calibration:** Record previous peak resonance moments to understand patterns in your perception and alignment.
- **Mindfulness Practices:** Brief meditation or focused breathing before execution can heighten awareness of both market signals and emotional state.
- **Dynamic Scaling:** Use small initial entries to test resonance, scaling in as alignment strengthens.

Examples of Resonant Moments

- During a breakout from consolidation, a trader notices increasing volume, steady momentum, and personal emotional calm. Entering now aligns perfectly with the market's energy.
- In a high-volatility environment, micro-trends within the larger movement appear consistent. Observing these early allows scaling in gradually as the market confirms direction.

- Conversely, attempting to act before volume or momentum confirms alignment may lead to forced trades and emotional strain, highlighting the importance of waiting for resonance.

Key Takeaways

- Peak resonance moments are a combination of **external market conditions and internal alignment**.
- Recognizing them requires **observation, mindfulness, and pattern awareness** rather than mechanical rule-following.
- Execution during these moments is fluid, deliberate, and aligned, reducing stress and improving decision quality.

"The market whispers its rhythm; the resonant trader hears, aligns, and moves effortlessly in time."

19.2 Avoiding Forced Action

Forced action in trading occurs when decisions are made under pressure, impatience, or emotional turbulence rather than in alignment with market rhythm. Acting without resonance often leads to **mistimed entries, overtrading, and emotional exhaustion**. Avoiding forced action is critical to maintaining flow, coherence, and sustainable performance.

Understanding Forced Action

Forced action typically arises from:

- **Impatience:** Feeling the need to "do something" when markets are calm or ambiguous.
- **Fear of Missing Out (FOMO):** Jumping into trades due to perceived opportunity rather than observable signals.
- **Overconfidence:** Believing intuition or past success justifies action without checking alignment.
- **External Pressure:** Market noise, peer behavior, or self-imposed performance expectations pushing premature execution.

Consequences of Forced Action

- Increased exposure to adverse price movement and unnecessary risk.
- Emotional imbalance leading to anxiety, frustration, or overreaction.
- Erosion of confidence and trust in one's judgment and trading framework.
- Disruption of long-term alignment and consistency.

Strategies to Avoid Forced Action

1. **Pause and Assess:** Before acting, pause to evaluate market conditions, personal emotional state, and alignment with trade plan.
2. **Observe Without Reacting:** Train the mind to monitor price movements and volume without feeling compelled to act immediately.
3. **Set Entry Conditions:** Predefine criteria for trade execution market patterns, volume confirmation, and emotional readiness. Only act when all criteria are satisfied.
4. **Incremental Engagement:** Use micro-entries to test resonance rather than committing full exposure prematurely.
5. **Mindfulness Practices:** Techniques such as deep breathing, short meditation, or focused attention can reduce impulsive tendencies and sharpen perception.
6. **Journaling and Reflection:** Record instances of forced action to identify triggers and improve future discipline.

Psychological Calibration

Maintaining a calm, observant state is essential:

- Recognize emotional signals such as tension, restlessness, or eagerness as indicators of potential forced action.
- Develop routines to reset alignment pause, breathe, and revisit trading objectives.
- Accept uncertainty as a natural part of markets; avoid substituting action for control.

Examples

- A trader observing a volatile breakout may feel compelled to enter immediately. By waiting for confirmation of volume and trend stability, execution aligns with resonance, reducing the risk of whipsaw.
- During low-volatility periods, impatience may trigger overtrading. Recognizing internal restlessness allows the trader to step back, preserving capital and emotional coherence.

Key Takeaways

- Forced action is a misalignment of internal state and market rhythm.
- Awareness, pre-defined entry conditions, and mindfulness are essential to prevent it.
- Avoiding forced action enhances **clarity, consistency, and performance**, transforming execution into a deliberate and resonant practice.

"The strongest trades are not those forced by impatience, but those born from alignment and resonance with the market's pulse."

19.3 Discipline in Waiting

In trading, waiting is often more important than acting. Discipline in waiting is the ability to **remain patient, observant, and aligned**, even when markets are tempting or emotionally charged. It is the foundation of flow-based execution: without the ability to wait for peak resonance, even the most sophisticated strategies fail.

The Value of Waiting

Waiting is not passivity; it is **active observation and preparation**. Properly waiting allows traders to:

- Enter trades only during moments of alignment between market conditions and internal readiness.
- Reduce exposure to noise and impulsive reactions.
- Preserve capital and emotional energy for high-probability opportunities.
- Strengthen confidence in their trading framework through consistent practice.

Challenges to Patience

Traders often struggle with waiting due to:

- **Impatience:** A desire to act because "something should be happening."
- **Fear of Missing Out (FOMO):** Anxiety over missed opportunities driving premature action.
- **Overconfidence:** Belief that intuition or past success justifies early entry.
- **Market Noise:** Fluctuations or commentary that create pressure to act.

Techniques to Cultivate Discipline in Waiting

1. **Pre-Defined Criteria:** Establish clear conditions for trade entry based on alignment with market rhythm and internal state. Only act when criteria are met.
2. **Mindful Observation:** Use meditation, breathing exercises, or focused attention to maintain calm and awareness while monitoring the market.
3. **Incremental Engagement:** Enter trades gradually when resonance begins to manifest, rather than fully committing prematurely.
4. **Journaling and Reflection:** Document periods of waiting, noting emotional triggers and lessons learned. This builds awareness and reinforces patience.
5. **Visualization:** Mentally rehearse waiting and disciplined execution to strengthen neural pathways for delayed action.

Practical Examples

- A trader observes a consolidation pattern forming before a potential breakout. Instead of acting on partial signals, they wait for clear volume confirmation, ensuring execution at peak resonance.
- During high-volatility sessions, small early moves may tempt action. By waiting for trend confirmation and emotional alignment, the trader avoids whipsaw and unnecessary losses.
- A trader feeling anxious due to market news uses a brief mindfulness exercise and observes without acting, preserving clarity and avoiding forced entries.

Key Takeaways

- Discipline in waiting is a proactive practice, not passivity.
- Waiting allows alignment of internal state with market rhythm, enabling flow-based execution.
- Mastery of patience leads to better timing, reduced emotional stress, and more consistent trading performance.

"In trading, patience is power; the market rewards those who wait in alignment, not those who act in haste."

Chapter 20

Measuring Resonance

Resonance is at the heart of flow-based trading it is the alignment between **market conditions, trader perception, and emotional state**. However, resonance is not always obvious or quantifiable. To trade effectively, it is essential to develop a framework for **measuring and monitoring resonance**, combining both subjective awareness and objective observation.

This chapter explores how traders can systematically assess resonance to improve decision-making. By measuring resonance, traders can **identify optimal entry points, maintain alignment, and calibrate their mental and emotional state**. This practice transforms execution from guesswork into a deliberate, repeatable process.

20.1 Subjective Indicators

Subjective indicators are **internal, personal signals** that reflect the trader's state of awareness, emotional coherence, and alignment with the market. Unlike charts or numerical metrics, these indicators are **felt rather than measured**, yet they are critical for identifying moments of true resonance.

The Role of Subjective Awareness

Subjective awareness allows traders to:

- Recognize subtle changes in attention, focus, and emotional balance.
- Differentiate between intuition aligned with market signals and impulsive reactions.
- Detect early signs of potential opportunities or misalignment before objective signals appear.

Key Subjective Indicators

Several internal cues can serve as reliable subjective indicators of resonance:

1. **Calm Focus:** A clear, steady mind indicates readiness for coherent action. Distraction, restlessness, or agitation signals misalignment.
2. **Emotional Coherence:** Harmonious emotional state confidence without overexcitement, alertness without fear supports optimal perception and decision-making.
3. **Heightened Sensory Awareness:** Subtle perception of market rhythm, such as noticing micro-movements, volume shifts, or momentum changes, often accompanies resonant states.
4. **Intuitive Clarity:** A sense of "knowing without thinking," where patterns and opportunities feel evident, is a hallmark of subjective resonance.
5. **Flow Feeling:** Time seems to expand or contract naturally, and observation feels effortless indicative of alignment with market energy.

Techniques to Enhance Subjective Indicators

- **Mindfulness Practices:** Regular meditation, breathing exercises, and body scans improve awareness and emotional coherence.
- **Focused Observation Exercises:** Tracking micro-movements in price or volume without acting strengthens sensitivity to subtle market cues.
- **Journaling Internal States:** Record emotional states, focus levels, and intuitive insights during trading sessions to identify patterns of resonance.
- **Pre-Trade Calibration:** Before entering the market, perform brief mental checks assess clarity, emotional stability, and readiness to act in alignment.

Practical Application

- A trader notices that during periods of calm focus, their entries coincide with profitable trends, while rushed or emotionally charged trades lead to poor outcomes.
- By journaling emotional states and perceived clarity, traders learn to recognize their own internal resonance patterns and time trades accordingly.
- Over time, subjective indicators act as an **early-warning system**, enabling anticipation of high-probability trading opportunities.

Key Takeaways

- Subjective indicators are internal cues reflecting alignment between the trader and market.
- Awareness, emotional coherence, and flow are critical signals for peak resonance moments.
- Developing these indicators requires mindfulness, observation, and reflective journaling, turning internal perception into actionable trading insight.

"The market speaks through subtle rhythms; the resonant trader listens first within."

20.2 Objective Metrics

Objective metrics provide **external, measurable signals** of market resonance that complement subjective awareness. These metrics quantify patterns, trends, and behaviors in the market, allowing traders to validate internal perceptions and align actions with market rhythm.

Purpose of Objective Metrics

While subjective indicators capture internal alignment, objective metrics:

- Offer **verifiable confirmation** of market conditions.
- Reduce reliance on intuition alone, minimizing emotional bias.
- Provide a framework for **systematic decision-making** across timeframes.
- Serve as benchmarks for tracking resonance over time.

Key Objective Metrics for Resonance

Several measurable indicators can help identify alignment between the trader and the market:

1. **Volume Patterns:** Sudden increases or decreases in trading volume often signal the amplification or fading of market energy. Resonant trades typically occur when volume confirms price movement rather than contradicts it.

2. **Volatility Measures:** Standard deviation, ATR (Average True Range), or implied volatility can indicate the amplitude of market "waves." Peaks in volatility may coincide with high-resonance moments or emotional extremes.

3. **Momentum Indicators:** Tools like RSI, MACD, or moving averages highlight the direction and strength of price action. Alignment is stronger when subjective resonance matches objective momentum signals.

4. **Market Breadth:** The proportion of advancing vs. declining assets or sectors reflects collective market energy and sentiment, confirming or contradicting perceived resonance.

5. **Correlation Metrics:** Cross-asset correlations help assess whether market energy is concentrated or dispersed, indicating systemic coherence or fragmentation.

Integrating Objective and Subjective Indicators

The most effective resonance measurement arises from **combining internal perception with external validation**:

- When subjective clarity aligns with objective volume and momentum signals, the probability of successful execution increases.
- Objective metrics act as **feedback loops**, refining awareness and training the mind to recognize resonance patterns.
- Misalignment between subjective feelings and objective data signals the need for caution, reflection, or adjustment.

Practical Examples

- A trader senses an intuitive pull toward a breakout trade. Checking volume and momentum confirms alignment, enabling confident execution.
- During low volatility, a trader's subjective calm may suggest readiness, but objective metrics show weak momentum, indicating that waiting is prudent.
- Correlation analysis reveals that a perceived opportunity in one asset coincides with systemic shifts across markets, validating the resonance signal.

Key Takeaways

- Objective metrics quantify market resonance and validate subjective perception.
- Volume, volatility, momentum, breadth, and correlation are primary measurable indicators.
- Effective trading integrates both **internal awareness and external signals** to enhance timing, confidence, and performance.

"Resonance is found where feeling meets measurement; intuition verified by the market's own pulse."

20.3 Journaling and Reflection

Journaling and reflection are the **bridge between perception, measurement, and learning**. They allow traders to record experiences, analyze patterns, and refine both subjective and objective indicators of resonance. Without structured reflection, insights from the market often remain fragmented and inconsistent.

Purpose of Journaling

The practice of journaling serves multiple critical purposes:

- **Capture Subjective States:** Document emotional and cognitive conditions at the time of trading to identify patterns of alignment or misalignment.
- **Track Objective Metrics:** Record market indicators such as volume, momentum, and correlations alongside trades to observe how they influence outcomes.
- **Enhance Self-Awareness:** Reflection allows recognition of biases, impulsive behavior, and recurring mistakes.
- **Reinforce Learning:** By reviewing entries, traders can strengthen their understanding of resonance patterns and refine execution strategies.

Components of an Effective Trading Journal

A comprehensive trading journal integrates **both internal and external observations**:

1. **Trade Details:** Asset, position size, entry and exit points, and timeframe.
2. **Subjective Observations:** Emotional state, level of focus, intuition, and perceived resonance.
3. **Objective Metrics:** Volume, volatility, momentum, correlations, or other relevant data points.
4. **Decision Rationale:** Why the trade was taken, what signals were considered, and how alignment was assessed.
5. **Outcome Analysis:** Profit/loss, quality of execution, and lessons learned.

Techniques for Effective Reflection

- **End-of-Day Review:** Reflect on all trades and non-trading observations. Identify moments of high resonance and moments where noise or emotional reactivity dominated.
- **Pattern Recognition:** Over weeks or months, analyze entries to discover recurring behavioral and market patterns.
- **Emotional Calibration Logs:** Record emotional fluctuations during market activity and link them to outcomes.
- **Visualization and Mind Mapping:** Map trade setups, resonance signals, and outcomes to visualize alignment and feedback loops.
- **Iterative Improvement:** Use insights from past trades to refine criteria for entry, exit, and timing, continuously enhancing both subjective and objective resonance measurement.

Practical Examples

- A trader documents that during high emotional arousal, entries are often misaligned with market momentum. Reflection leads to pre-trade calming routines, improving future alignment.
- Journaling reveals that trades taken during low volatility periods feel subjectively "aligned," but objective metrics indicate weak resonance, prompting better timing strategies.
- By combining emotional logs with volume and momentum charts, a trader learns to anticipate micro-waves of market energy, improving entry precision.

Key Takeaways

- Journaling and reflection convert experience into structured knowledge, enhancing resonance awareness.
- Both subjective and objective elements should be recorded to create a holistic view of market interaction.
- Regular reflection enables continuous improvement, helping traders **hone intuition, recognize patterns, and execute with clarity**.

"The market teaches, but only the reflective student learns; journaling turns perception into wisdom."

Chapter 21

Avoiding Disconnection

Trading is not only a technical or analytical exercise; it is an **ongoing dialogue between the trader and the market**. Disconnection occurs when the trader's perception, emotions, or actions drift out of alignment with the market's rhythm. Even highly skilled traders can experience periods of misalignment, leading to impulsive decisions, missed opportunities, or repeated mistakes.

This chapter explores how to **recognize, prevent, and correct disconnection**. By understanding the signs of misalignment, implementing daily calibration routines, and managing emotional energy effectively, traders can maintain a consistent state of resonance. Avoiding disconnection is essential for sustaining clarity, confidence, and flow, ensuring that both subjective intuition and objective metrics remain synchronized with market dynamics.

21.1 Symptoms of Misalignment

Misalignment occurs when a trader's mind, emotions, or actions drift out of sync with the market's rhythm. Recognizing these symptoms early is critical for preventing poor decisions, emotional stress, and loss of confidence. Misalignment can manifest cognitively, emotionally, and behaviorally, often signaling that the trader is disconnected from the flow of the market.

Cognitive Symptoms

- **Overthinking and Analysis Paralysis:** Excessive mental deliberation without decisive action indicates that perception and decision-making are no longer aligned.
- **Distorted Risk Perception:** Misjudging probabilities, overestimating potential losses, or underestimating opportunities suggests cognitive dissonance.

- **Focus Fragmentation:** Difficulty maintaining attention on relevant price action or market signals often reflects internal distraction or mental fatigue.
- **Rigid Thinking:** Clinging to preconceived notions or narratives despite contradictory market evidence indicates disconnection from objective reality.

Emotional Symptoms

- **Excessive Fear or Anxiety:** Heightened worry or dread about market moves can cause hesitation or reactionary trades.
- **Overconfidence or Euphoria:** Inflated confidence may lead to impulsive entries, ignoring objective signals or risk parameters.
- **Emotional Volatility:** Rapid swings between hope, fear, and frustration reveal a lack of emotional regulation.
- **Irritability and Restlessness:** Difficulty sitting through trades or waiting for optimal setups often accompanies misalignment.

Behavioral Symptoms

- **Chasing Trades:** Entering positions impulsively due to fear of missing out (FOMO) rather than signal alignment.
- **Overtrading or Undertrading:** Excessive or insufficient activity reflects poor calibration with market energy.
- **Ignoring Rules or Systems:** Deviating from trading plans or established frameworks indicates a disconnect between knowledge and execution.
- **Reactive Decision-Making:** Responding to minor fluctuations or noise rather than waiting for resonance signals demonstrates misalignment.

Early Warning Signals

Traders can monitor subtle signs that misalignment is developing:

- Feeling mentally "foggy" or emotionally drained before or during trading.
- Noticing repeated small mistakes or missed opportunities despite objective signals.
- Experiencing impatience or restlessness during market pauses.
- Sensory or perceptual dullness, such as missing volume spikes, momentum shifts, or micro-oscillations.

Key Takeaways

- Misalignment can manifest cognitively, emotionally, and behaviorally; early recognition is crucial.
- Symptoms such as overthinking, fear, euphoria, reactive trading, and rule-breaking indicate disconnection.
- Monitoring subtle early warning signals allows traders to take corrective action, recalibrating mind, emotion, and behavior to restore resonance.

"Awareness of misalignment is the first step toward restoring flow; the market mirrors the state of the trader."

21.2 Emotional Energy Management

Emotional energy is the **driving force behind perception, decision-making, and action** in trading. Maintaining a balanced, regulated emotional state is critical for staying aligned with the market's rhythm. Mismanaged emotional energy leads to impulsive decisions, overtrading, or complete disconnection from market signals.

This section explores strategies for **monitoring, regulating, and optimizing emotional energy** to sustain flow, coherence, and long-term trading performance.

Understanding Emotional Energy in Trading

- **Energy States Influence Perception:** Emotional highs (euphoria) and lows (fear, anxiety) distort how traders interpret signals and assess risk.
- **Resonance Requires Emotional Balance:** High alignment with market energy occurs when emotional energy is neither excessive nor depleted.
- **Energy as a Limited Resource:** Trading while fatigued, stressed, or distracted reduces attention, increases reactionary behavior, and diminishes resonance.

Techniques for Managing Emotional Energy

1. **Pre-Trading Preparation:**
    - Engage in short mindfulness or breathing exercises to calm the nervous system.

- Review trading plans and objectives to anchor attention and intention.
- Set emotional check-ins before the session to identify current energy state.

2. **During Trading:**
   - Monitor physiological cues such as heart rate, tension, or shallow breathing as signals of emotional drift.
   - Pause or step away if emotional intensity spikes reactive trades rarely align with market resonance.
   - Maintain focus on pre-defined signals and frameworks rather than external noise.

3. **Post-Trading Reflection:**
   - Document emotional states alongside trades in a journal.
   - Identify patterns of energy depletion or surges and correlate with outcomes.
   - Plan recovery and recalibration routines, such as rest, exercise, or meditation.

Sustaining Long-Term Emotional Energy

- **Regular Rest and Recovery:** Avoid trading while fatigued; sleep, breaks, and mental downtime are essential.
- **Physical Wellness:** Nutrition, hydration, and exercise influence emotional regulation and cognitive performance.
- **Energy Boundaries:** Limit exposure to emotionally draining market periods or overexposure to high-volatility sessions.
- **Support Systems:** Engaging with mentors, peers, or coaches can help process emotional experiences and sustain resilience.

Practical Exercises

- Conduct a daily "energy audit" before and after trading sessions, rating focus, stress, and emotional clarity.
- Implement short breathing or grounding exercises during periods of heightened market volatility.
- Pair journaling with physiological monitoring (heart rate, tension) to correlate emotional energy with trading outcomes.

Key Takeaways

- Emotional energy directly influences market alignment, decision quality, and execution.
- Managing energy involves preparation, active monitoring, reflection, and long-term wellness practices.
- By sustaining emotional coherence, traders enhance their ability to detect subtle signals, maintain flow, and avoid disconnection.

"Emotional energy is the currency of resonance; manage it wisely, and the market becomes a reflection of your clarity."

Part IV

Mastery and Integration

Chapter 22

Trading as Dialogue with Uncertainty

Markets are inherently uncertain and unpredictable, yet traders continually seek patterns, signals, and strategies to navigate them. This chapter reframes trading as a **dynamic dialogue between the trader and the market**, rather than a one-sided pursuit of profit. By embracing uncertainty as an active participant in the process, traders can cultivate awareness, adaptability, and resilience.

The concept of trading as a dialogue emphasizes that outcomes are not solely determined by market mechanics, but also by the trader's perception, decisions, and alignment. Every interaction every observation, decision, and action affects the unfolding market reality, creating a continuous feedback loop between observer and system.

22.1 Markets as Co-Created Reality

Markets are not merely mechanical systems responding to supply and demand; they are **living, emergent phenomena shaped by the collective cognition, emotions, and actions of all participants**. Each trader's perception, decision, and behavior contributes to the formation of market reality, creating a **co-created ecosystem** in which individual and collective actions interact dynamically.

The Interplay of Individual and Collective Behavior

Every trader is both an observer and a participant. Observing price movements, news, and signals influences the trader's decisions, which in turn contribute to market movements. This interplay forms a **feedback loop**, where the market reflects not only fundamental or technical factors but also the **emotional and cognitive states of participants**.

- **Belief Amplification:** Shared beliefs such as bullish sentiment or fear of decline can amplify price movements, sometimes independent of fundamental valuation.
- **Herding Effects:** Collective imitation leads to emergent trends, momentum waves, or cascading reactions, demonstrating that the market's behavior is not just the sum of individual rationality but of **shared perception**.
- **Observer Participation:** Every trade placed, even by a single participant, subtly alters the probabilities and emotional landscape of the market.

Perception Shapes Reality

Traders interpret the same data differently, creating multiple narratives around the same event. Over time, dominant narratives influence behavior:

- News events or economic reports are filtered through collective perception, sometimes causing exaggerated reactions.
- Expectations of other participants' behavior become self-fulfilling prophecies, further entwining perception and price movement.
- Market anomalies, corrections, or bubbles can often be traced to **discrepancies between collective perception and underlying reality**, showing the subjective nature of market "truth."

Practical Implications for Traders

Understanding markets as co-created realities changes how one approaches decision-making:

- Recognize that your **beliefs and actions influence the market**, and act with awareness rather than reactively.
- Monitor **collective sentiment and narrative shifts** as early indicators of emerging trends or reversals.
- Develop **flexibility in interpretation**, acknowledging that multiple realities coexist depending on participants' mental models.
- Engage in reflective practice, journaling not only trades but the **emotional and cognitive context** in which decisions were made.

Key Takeaways

- Markets are **co-created by all participant**; your actions influence and are influenced by collective behavior.
- Shared beliefs, emotions, and narratives can amplify or dampen market movements, independent of fundamentals.
- Awareness of this co-creative process allows traders to **align perception, emotion, and action**, enhancing decision-making under uncertainty.

"The market is not just observed it is lived, shaped, and co-created by every participant's perception and action."

22.2 Accepting Uncertainty Without Paralysis

Uncertainty is the **inherent condition of markets**. Prices fluctuate, events unfold unpredictably, and outcomes are never fully known in advance. For traders, accepting uncertainty is not merely a philosophical exercise it is a **practical necessity**. Failing to accept uncertainty often leads to **analysis paralysis**, emotional exhaustion, or reactive decision-making. This section explores how to embrace uncertainty constructively while maintaining clarity, focus, and effective action.

The Nature of Market Uncertainty

- **Incomplete Information:** Traders rarely have full visibility into all market participants' intentions, macroeconomic shifts, or unexpected events.
- **Dynamic Interactions:** The market is a constantly evolving system, where each participant's action influences outcomes in real time.
- **Emergent Phenomena:** Sudden trends, reversals, or volatility spikes often arise from complex interactions that are impossible to predict with certainty.

Why Uncertainty Causes Paralysis

- **Overanalysis:** Attempting to account for every possible scenario leads to delayed decisions and missed opportunities.
- **Fear of Mistakes:** Anxiety about making the wrong move can immobilize traders, resulting in hesitation and inaction.

- **Need for Control:** A desire to eliminate risk entirely conflicts with the reality of unpredictable markets, creating stress and indecision.

Strategies for Embracing Uncertainty

1. **Focus on Probabilities, Not Certainties:**
    - Evaluate trades in terms of likelihoods and potential outcomes rather than expecting perfect prediction.
    - Accept that losses are inevitable and that risk is a feature, not a flaw, of trading.
2. **Develop Flexible Frameworks:**
    - Use adaptable strategies that allow you to respond to changing market conditions.
    - Incorporate contingency plans, adjustable risk parameters, and exit rules.
3. **Cultivate Emotional Resilience:**
    - Practice mindfulness, deep breathing, or brief pauses before executing trades to prevent emotional overreaction.
    - Normalize uncertainty as part of the trading process, reducing fear and anxiety.
4. **Incremental Decision-Making:**
    - Take small, deliberate actions rather than committing fully under high uncertainty.
    - Observe how the market responds and adjust decisions accordingly, creating a feedback-informed approach.

Practical Exercises

- Maintain a journal of uncertain trading scenarios, documenting your thoughts, emotional state, and decisions.
- Create "what-if" simulations to practice responding to unexpected market events without panic.
- Schedule reflection periods post-trading to review how uncertainty was managed and identify opportunities for improvement.

Key Takeaways

- Uncertainty is inherent in markets and cannot be eliminated accepting it is essential.
- Paralysis arises from overanalysis, fear, and the illusion of control.
- Probabilistic thinking, flexible frameworks, emotional resilience, and incremental action allow traders to **act decisively in the face of uncertainty**.

"Uncertainty is not a barrier it is the canvas on which skill, awareness, and adaptability paint opportunity."

22.3 Adaptive Mindset Practices

In the ever-changing landscape of markets, a rigid mindset can hinder performance, while an adaptive mindset enables traders to **respond effectively, learn continuously, and maintain alignment with market dynamics**. Developing adaptive practices allows traders to navigate uncertainty, capitalize on emergent opportunities, and maintain emotional and cognitive coherence.

Core Principles of an Adaptive Mindset

- **Flexibility over Rigidity:** Adaptability means adjusting strategies, perspectives, and actions as conditions evolve rather than clinging to fixed assumptions or methods.
- **Learning Orientation:** Treat every market interaction as feedback. Profitable or losing trades are opportunities to refine understanding, improve mental models, and calibrate perception.
- **Resilience Under Stress:** Adaptive traders maintain composure in volatile or unexpected situations, preventing reactive behavior and maintaining clarity.
- **Proactive Awareness:** Anticipating potential market shifts, identifying early signals, and adjusting mental frameworks in real time enhances responsiveness.

Techniques to Cultivate Adaptability

1. **Dynamic Mental Models:**
    - Maintain multiple explanatory frameworks for price movement (fundamentals, sentiment, technical patterns).

- Switch between models as conditions change, avoiding overreliance on a single perspective.

2. **Scenario Planning and Simulation:**
    - Regularly practice "what-if" scenarios to prepare for unexpected events.
    - Visualize different outcomes and determine flexible responses, improving mental agility.

3. **Reflective Journaling:**
    - Record decisions, thought processes, emotional states, and observed market conditions.
    - Analyze patterns over time to identify rigid habits or biases, and consciously adjust behavior.

4. **Incremental Experimentation:**
    - Test new strategies or approaches in controlled increments rather than fully committing.
    - Observe outcomes and iterate, creating a cycle of continuous adaptation.

5. **Emotional Calibration Exercises:**
    - Use mindfulness, breathing, or short meditative pauses to reset emotional state when facing market shocks.
    - Train the mind to separate observation from reaction, allowing deliberate decision-making even under stress.

Integrating Adaptation into Daily Practice

- Begin each session by assessing your mental, emotional, and physical readiness to adapt.
- Set flexible trading objectives that prioritize alignment and learning over rigid profit targets.
- Conduct post-session reviews focusing on adaptive behavior: what adjustments were made, what worked, and what can be improved.

Key Takeaways

- Markets are dynamic; adaptive traders embrace change rather than resist it.
- Developing an adaptive mindset requires flexibility, reflection, experimentation, and emotional calibration.

- By integrating adaptive practices, traders can transform uncertainty from a source of stress into an arena for learning, insight, and strategic advantage.

"Adaptability is not merely a skill it is the art of coexisting with uncertainty, turning each shift in the market into an opportunity for insight and aligned action."

Chapter 23

Synchronization of Mind and Market

Trading is not only a matter of analysis and strategy it is fundamentally an exercise in **alignment between the trader's internal state and the external dynamics of the market**. Just as musicians synchronize to a shared rhythm or dancers respond intuitively to one another, traders who cultivate awareness, presence, and resonance can achieve a state of **flow**, where perception, decision-making, and execution harmonize seamlessly with market movement.

23.1 Flow and Intuition Alignment

Flow is the state in which a trader's **mind, emotions, and actions operate in seamless harmony with the market's dynamics**. In this state, perception becomes heightened, decisions are made effortlessly, and execution is precise. Achieving flow requires both self-awareness and the ability to interpret subtle market cues intuitively.

The Nature of Flow in Trading

Flow is characterized by:

- **Focused Awareness:** Complete attention on the present moment, minimizing distraction and mental noise.
- **Effortless Action:** Decisions and actions arise naturally from observation and understanding, rather than from forced analysis.
- **Timely Responsiveness:** Actions are executed in rhythm with market movements, capturing opportunities and avoiding reactive mistakes.

Flow is not randomness or luck it is the result of **preparation, practice, and attunement** to both internal and external signals.

Intuition as a Guide

Intuition in trading is the ability to sense **patterns, sentiment, and probability shifts** before they fully manifest in price:

- Develop intuition through repeated exposure to market patterns, journaling, and reflection.
- Learn to differentiate intuitive signals from impulsive reactions. Intuition is subtle, consistent, and often accompanied by a calm clarity rather than emotional agitation.
- Trusting intuition does not mean abandoning analysis; rather, it complements analytical frameworks with **pre-conscious pattern recognition.**

Techniques to Cultivate Flow and Intuition

1. **Mindfulness Practice:** Engage in brief meditative or breathing exercises before trading to center attention and reduce emotional volatility.
2. **Pattern Immersion:** Review historical charts, replay market scenarios, and observe sentiment shifts to train subconscious recognition of market rhythms.
3. **Journaling Insights:** Record not only trades but the **emotional and cognitive context** at the time of decisions, reinforcing intuitive learning.
4. **Small Incremental Practice:** Begin with low-risk trades or simulations to practice aligning observation, intuition, and action before scaling to higher stakes.

Practical Application

- Identify moments when the market's movement resonates with your analysis and emotional state.
- Avoid forcing trades when intuition and flow are misaligned; recognize these as signals to pause and recalibrate.
- Reflect daily on moments of flow: what conditions, mindset, and signals contributed to alignment? Use these reflections to enhance future trading sessions.

Key Takeaways

- Flow is the alignment of mind, emotion, and action with market dynamics.
- Intuition arises from deep familiarity and reflective practice, guiding timely and precise decisions.
- Consistent cultivation of flow and intuition transforms trading from reaction to resonance, increasing clarity, confidence, and effectiveness.

"Flow is the moment when observation becomes understanding, and understanding becomes action without hesitation."

23.2 Collective Rhythm and Decision Harmony

Beyond individual alignment, the market is a **shared cognitive and emotional system** where the actions, expectations, and sentiments of countless participants interact continuously. Recognizing and synchronizing with this **collective rhythm** allows traders to make decisions that are not only personally coherent but also **in harmony with the broader market flow**.

The Market as a Collective System

- The market can be thought of as a **nervous system**, where each participant contributes signals, amplifications, and feedback loops.
- Price movements reflect aggregated decisions, emotional waves, and shared beliefs, creating rhythms that repeat across timeframes.
- Understanding these rhythms enables traders to anticipate potential reactions and position themselves in **resonance rather than against the collective momentum**.

Synchronization with Collective Sentiment

- Observe broad sentiment indicators, such as volume surges, volatility shifts, and news-driven reactions.
- Detect subtle alignment or dissonance between your own perception and the collective market mood.
- Aim to act in moments where personal analysis, emotional state, and collective market signals converge.

Principles of Decision Harmony

1. **Listen Before Acting:** Monitor both quantitative signals and qualitative cues from market participants to sense emerging trends.

2. **Adapt, Don't Force:** Avoid imposing decisions when collective momentum is contrary to your position; instead, adjust entries, exits, or risk exposure.

3. **Anticipate Feedback Loops:** Recognize that your own actions influence the collective, creating loops that can amplify or dampen price moves.

4. **Maintain Emotional Coherence:** Emotional misalignment with the market often leads to premature or delayed actions. Staying calm enhances both perception and timing.

Practical Techniques for Harmony

- **Market Flow Mapping:** Track trends, sentiment oscillations, and volatility clusters to identify periods of collective alignment.

- **Simulation and Observation:** Use historical data to simulate collective responses to similar scenarios and refine anticipation skills.

- **Reflective Practice:** After each trading session, review moments where your decisions either aligned or conflicted with the broader market rhythm. Learn from both.

Key Takeaways

- Markets are collective organisms; individual trades are most effective when synchronized with broader sentiment and momentum.

- Decision harmony combines personal flow, intuition, and awareness of collective rhythms.

- Practicing alignment with the market's collective frequency enhances timing, reduces conflict, and improves overall trading effectiveness.

"True mastery emerges when the trader's mind dances in step with the market's collective heartbeat."

Chapter 24

Beyond Winning and Losing

Traditional trading often emphasizes profits and losses as the primary measure of success. However, this focus can obscure the deeper purpose of market engagement: **developing awareness, understanding patterns of behavior, and cultivating mastery over perception and decision-making**. True trading excellence is not defined solely by short-term gains but by the trader's ability to navigate uncertainty, adapt continuously, and integrate learning from each market interaction.

24.1 Trading as Awareness Practice

Trading is more than a pursuit of profit; it is fundamentally a **practice of self-awareness, perception, and reflection**. Each interaction with the market provides an opportunity to observe not only price action but also **one's own cognitive and emotional responses**. By approaching trading as a conscious practice, traders can develop clarity, discipline, and adaptability that extend far beyond individual trades.

The Mindful Trader

- A mindful trader cultivates **present-moment awareness**, observing market developments without immediate judgment or impulsive reaction.
- Awareness extends to **internal states**: recognizing fear, hope, overconfidence, or hesitation as signals rather than obstacles.
- This practice allows the trader to **differentiate signal from noise**, identifying meaningful patterns while avoiding reactionary decisions driven by transient emotions.

Observing Patterns of Behavior

- Markets are reflections of collective cognition and emotion. By observing recurring behavioral patterns both in oneself and across the market a trader can anticipate probable outcomes with greater clarity.
- Journaling trades, thoughts, and emotional states strengthens **pattern recognition** at a psychological and behavioral level.
- Reflection enables a trader to distinguish between **habitual reactions** and informed decisions aligned with strategy and flow.

Integrating Awareness Into Action

1. Pause before executing trades to **assess both market signals and emotional readiness**.
2. Use introspective questions: "Am I reacting to fear or opportunity? Is my analysis aligned with what the market is signaling?"
3. Apply calibrated decisions that reflect both **internal coherence** and **external market dynamics**, rather than impulsive judgments.

Benefits of Awareness Practice

- Reduces emotional overreactions and impulsive trading.
- Improves timing, entry, and exit decisions through heightened perception of market flow.
- Encourages continuous learning and self-improvement, making every trade a feedback loop for personal and professional growth.

Key Takeaways

- Trading as a practice emphasizes **observation, reflection, and alignment** over immediate results.
- Awareness allows traders to **engage the market with clarity, discipline, and purpose**, creating conditions for sustainable mastery.
- By treating each trade as a learning opportunity, traders cultivate both **psychological resilience** and **strategic insight**.

"Profit is a byproduct; awareness is the true currency of the trader."

24.2 Long-Term Adaptation vs Short-Term Outcomes

While short-term profits and losses often dominate a trader's attention, sustainable trading success relies on **long-term adaptation and continuous learning**. Focusing solely on immediate outcomes can lead to emotional reactivity, overtrading, and suboptimal decisions. By prioritizing adaptation, traders develop **resilience, insight, and mastery over both markets and themselves.**

The Pitfalls of Short-Term Focus

- **Emotional Volatility:** Overemphasis on individual wins or losses amplifies fear and greed, disrupting flow and alignment.
- **Reactive Behavior:** Short-term pressure encourages impulsive trades, forcing actions that conflict with strategy or intuition.
- **Limited Learning:** Obsessing over immediate results can obscure the patterns and lessons that accumulate over time, preventing growth of market understanding.

Principles of Long-Term Adaptation

- **Process Over Outcome:** Prioritize adherence to disciplined frameworks, emotional calibration, and consistent reflection over the profit or loss of a single trade.
- **Cumulative Learning:** Each market interaction provides feedback successes, mistakes, and near-misses all contribute to the trader's evolving skill set.
- **Flexibility and Evolution:** Adapt strategies and mental models in response to new patterns, market structures, or personal insights, rather than rigidly repeating past approaches.

Strategies for Sustainable Adaptation

1. **Journaling and Reflection:** Document not only trades but also **mental state, decision rationale, and observed market behavior** to identify trends in personal performance.
2. **Periodic Review:** Regularly assess strategies and results in a broader context to determine whether decisions are aligned with long-term goals.

3. **Iterative Experimentation:** Test new approaches in small, controlled environments to learn without risking significant capital, refining methods based on feedback loops.

4. **Emotional Calibration:** Maintain awareness of psychological biases and emotional states, using them as signals for recalibration rather than triggers for impulsive action.

Balancing Short-Term and Long-Term Perspectives

- Short-term outcomes are unavoidable, but they should be **interpreted as data points** rather than absolute judgments of ability or strategy.
- Cultivate a mindset where **every trade contributes to skill growth**, emotional discipline, and understanding of market dynamics.
- Decisions are most effective when grounded in **long-term alignment**, integrating personal mastery, flow, and market resonance.

Key Takeaways

- Sustainable trading depends on **continuous adaptation**, not the pursuit of immediate results.
- Viewing trading through the lens of **long-term learning** reduces emotional reactivity and increases strategic clarity.
- By balancing short-term outcomes with long-term goals, traders develop **resilience, insight, and mastery** that compound over time.

"Short-term wins fade, but long-term adaptation builds enduring mastery."

Chapter 25

The Market as a Mirror of Consciousness

Markets are more than mechanisms for exchanging assets they are **reflective surfaces for human consciousness**. Every price movement, wave of sentiment, and collective reaction provides insight into **our own beliefs, biases, and emotional patterns**. By engaging with the market thoughtfully, traders can use it as a tool for **self-reflection, ethical decision-making, and psychological growth**.

25.1 Self-Reflection Through Market Interaction

Every interaction with the market is not only a financial event but also a **psychological and emotional experiment**. The market responds to collective behavior, sentiment, and perception, and in turn, traders' responses reflect their own **mental models, biases, and emotional patterns**. By observing these reactions carefully, one can gain profound insight into the inner workings of their own mind.

This section emphasizes the importance of **viewing trading as a mirror** where gains, losses, hesitation, or impulsive actions reveal deeper truths about one's cognitive and emotional state. Key aspects include:

- **Awareness of Emotional Triggers:** Identifying moments of fear, overconfidence, or doubt as signals of personal biases rather than purely market conditions.
- **Cognitive Patterns:** Recognizing recurring thought processes, narratives, and assumptions that shape decisions and influence risk perception.

- **Behavioral Feedback:** Understanding how repeated responses to market movements reveal habitual reactions, enabling conscious adjustments.
- **Learning Through Reflection:** Journaling, reviewing trades, and analyzing emotional states help transform experience into **self-knowledge and mental calibration**.

By cultivating this reflective approach, traders can **decouple automatic reactions from deliberate decisions**, enhancing clarity, resilience, and alignment with both the market and personal values. The market thus becomes a **dynamic feedback loop**, offering continuous opportunities for self-understanding and mastery.

25.2 Ethical and Psychological Growth

Trading is not merely a technical or financial exercise it is also a **practice in ethical decision-making and psychological development**. Each choice a trader makes carries consequences, both for personal outcomes and for the broader market ecosystem. By consciously engaging with the ethical and psychological dimensions of trading, individuals can cultivate **integrity, resilience, and long-term mastery**.

Integrating Ethics into Market Decisions

- Recognize the impact of decisions on others: even subtle trades can influence sentiment, liquidity, and market dynamics.
- Develop a framework of **personal values** to guide decisions, ensuring alignment between financial goals and ethical principles.
- Avoid short-term gains that compromise long-term integrity; prioritize **responsible and sustainable engagement** with the market.

Psychological Growth Through Market Interaction

- Treat losses, mistakes, and volatility as opportunities for **self-examination and learning** rather than sources of shame or frustration.
- Use trading as a mirror to uncover **biases, fears, and blind spots**, which can then be consciously addressed.
- Foster **emotional regulation** and mental discipline, transforming reactive impulses into deliberate, coherent action.

Practical Approaches

1. Maintain a **reflective journal** documenting not only trade outcomes but also emotional states, decision rationale, and ethical considerations.

2. Periodically review trading behavior in light of personal values, asking: "Are my actions aligned with my long-term principles and goals?"

3. Integrate mindfulness, meditation, or contemplative practices to enhance awareness, emotional stability, and ethical clarity in high-pressure situations.

Key Takeaways

- Trading is a vehicle for both **financial and personal development** when approached with intentionality.

- Ethical awareness ensures decisions are **aligned with values**, reducing regret and fostering trust in oneself and others.

- Psychological growth emerges from **reflective practice**, self-awareness, and continuous adaptation, creating a resilient and mature trader.

"The market teaches not only what to trade, but who we are and who we aspire to become."

Chapter 26

The Resonant Trader

The culmination of the concepts explored throughout this book is the development of the **Resonant Trader** an individual who harmonizes observation, emotional intelligence, cognitive clarity, and probabilistic reasoning into a coherent and sustainable approach to the markets. A resonant trader does not merely react to price action; they **flow with the market**, sense subtle shifts, and make decisions that are aligned with both internal coherence and external signals.

This chapter focuses on **integration and mastery**. It highlights how observation, awareness, flow, probability assessment, and emotional calibration converge to create a trader capable of sustained performance, adaptability, and resilience. The principles outlined here are not just techniques they represent a **philosophical and practical framework** for achieving both psychological and operational alignment in trading.

26.1 Integration of Observation, Flow, Probability, and Emotion

At the core of resonant trading lies the **integration of multiple dimensions of awareness**: the precision of observation, the intuitive rhythm of flow, probabilistic thinking, and emotional calibration. Each component contributes to a trader's ability to respond to the market **with clarity, adaptability, and coherence**, transforming complexity into actionable insight.

Observation: Seeing Beyond Price

Observation is more than monitoring charts or indicators it is a **deep, attentive engagement** with the market's movements, sentiment, and micro-signals. By cultivating heightened observational skills, traders can detect subtle shifts in liquidity, order flow, and behavioral patterns that precede larger price movements.

- **Micro-Signals:** Identifying small fluctuations, emotional imbalances, or volume anomalies that hint at impending moves.
- **Contextual Awareness:** Placing each signal within the broader market, macroeconomic, and behavioral context.
- **Continuous Feedback:** Treating observation as a dynamic feedback loop, where every interaction informs subsequent perception and decisions.

Flow: Aligning Mind with Market Rhythm

Flow is the **state of effortless engagement**, where a trader's cognitive, emotional, and physical faculties are harmonized with the market's dynamics. Flow enables rapid recognition of patterns, intuitive decision-making, and resistance to reactive impulses.

- Entering flow requires **emotional balance, mental clarity, and confidence** in one's framework.
- Flow enhances sensitivity to resonance and the subtle energy of price movements.
- Maintaining flow over multiple timeframes strengthens adaptive skill and reduces the impact of volatility-induced stress.

Probability: Thinking in Ranges and Likelihoods

A resonant trader integrates **probabilistic reasoning** into every decision. Recognizing that no trade is certain, probability allows for **risk calibration, expectation management, and resilience** in the face of market uncertainty.

- Estimating likelihoods based on historical patterns, current market conditions, and behavioral signals.
- Balancing expected value against risk to make consistent, rational choices.
- Avoiding overconfidence or deterministic thinking that can disrupt flow and emotional stability.

Emotion: Calibrated Energy and Awareness

Emotional regulation is central to resonant trading. Emotions act as both **informational signals and potential distortions**. The key lies in recognizing and **aligning emotional energy** with decision-making, rather than suppressing or ignoring it.

- Awareness of fear, greed, excitement, and doubt as **inputs, not controllers**, of behavior.
- Using emotional cues to enhance sensitivity to market resonance and timing.
- Cultivating resilience and equanimity to sustain long-term engagement and learning.

Synthesis: The Resonant Trader in Action

Integration means **weaving observation, flow, probability, and emotion into a coherent decision-making framework**:

1. Observe subtle market signals with attention and context.
2. Enter flow, aligning intuition and cognitive faculties with market rhythm.
3. Apply probabilistic assessment to evaluate likely outcomes and manage risk.
4. Calibrate emotional state to maintain coherence and responsiveness.
5. Execute decisions that are adaptive, informed, and aligned with long-term objectives.

When these dimensions function in concert, the trader is not merely reacting to the market they are **co-creating outcomes, continuously learning, and operating from a state of resonant alignment**.

"Mastery is not in control over the market, but in harmony with its rhythm, guided by awareness, insight, and emotional clarity."

26.2 Principles for Sustained Mastery

Achieving mastery in trading is not a destination but a continuous process of **alignment, learning, and adaptation**. The Resonant Trader sustains high-level performance by integrating practical habits, philosophical insight, and psychological resilience. This section outlines key principles that underpin long-term mastery and consistency in dynamic markets.

1. Continuous Observation and Reflection

- Regularly review market interactions to identify patterns, biases, and emotional triggers.
- Use journaling and post-trade analysis as tools to enhance **self-awareness** and decision quality.

- Treat every market scenario profit or loss as an opportunity to refine understanding and improve mental calibration.

2. Alignment of Mind, Emotion, and Action

- Maintain coherence between thoughts, feelings, and execution to reduce reactionary mistakes.
- Develop routines that foster emotional balance, such as mindfulness, reflection, or pre-market preparation.
- Recognize that sustained mastery is not about suppressing emotions but **harnessing them as informational signals**.

3. Probabilistic and Adaptive Thinking

- Embrace uncertainty as a constant, and evaluate trades in terms of probabilities rather than certainties.
- Adapt strategies to changing conditions while adhering to core principles.
- Avoid rigid adherence to any single framework; instead, cultivate **flexibility guided by patterns, resonance, and experience**.

4. Flow and Timing

- Recognize and act during peak resonance moments, when observation, intuition, and emotional clarity align.
- Practice patience and restraint to avoid forced actions or overtrading.
- Use periods of calm or market noise as opportunities for **internal calibration and preparation** rather than impulsive engagement.

5. Lifelong Learning and Iterative Improvement

- Treat trading as a **practice in growth**, where continuous learning and refinement are more valuable than short-term outcomes.
- Incorporate feedback loops, reflective exercises, and evolving mental models into everyday practice.
- Recognize that mastery is a dynamic state; it requires humility, curiosity, and consistent effort over time.

6. Ethical and Conscious Practice

- Align decisions with personal values and ethical principles to maintain trust in oneself and the trading ecosystem.
- Acknowledge the broader impact of actions on markets and fellow participants.
- Sustain motivation and clarity by integrating purpose and meaning into trading practice.

Key Takeaways

By integrating these principles, the Resonant Trader achieves:

- Coherence between observation, emotion, and execution.
- Adaptability to market fluctuations without losing alignment or composure.
- Continuous growth in skill, insight, and self-awareness.
- A sustainable and resilient approach to trading that transcends short-term results.

"Mastery is measured not by isolated wins or losses, but by the consistent ability to act with awareness, alignment, and resilience across the unfolding rhythm of the market."

Glossary

This glossary provides clear definitions and conceptual explanations of key terms used throughout this book. Mastery of these concepts is essential for understanding the frameworks, exercises, and mental models presented, as well as for developing the mindset of a resonant trader.

Resonance

Resonance refers to the amplification or alignment of energy between market participants, price movements, and trader perception. When multiple traders' actions, emotions, or cognitive states synchronize, the market exhibits patterns of coherence that can **magnify trends and signals**. Recognizing resonance allows traders to identify moments of **high probability alignment** between internal and external dynamics.

Amplitude

Amplitude describes the magnitude or intensity of market movements. It reflects the **collective emotional energy** of participants. High amplitude typically corresponds to strong sentiment, momentum, or volatility, while low amplitude indicates calm or indecision. Understanding amplitude helps traders gauge the **strength and sustainability of trends**.

Emotional Frequency

Emotional frequency captures the characteristic emotional "vibration" or state driving trader behavior at a given moment. Frequencies can include fear, greed, hope, excitement, or calm awareness. Emotional frequency influences **market micro-oscillations, timing, and decision-making**, making it a critical dimension for sensing resonance and flow.

Coherence

Coherence is the alignment between a trader's perception, emotion, cognition, and action with the underlying market dynamics. High coherence allows traders to make **informed, confident, and adaptive decisions**, while low coherence often results in reactionary trades, indecision, or emotional overreactions. Maintaining coherence is central to the **Resonant Trader framework**.

Feedback Loops

Feedback loops are cyclic interactions where actions influence outcomes, which in turn influence future actions. In markets, feedback loops can be:

- **Constructive:** Amplifying trends and reinforcing alignment between market sentiment and price action.
- **Destructive:** Creating volatility, misalignment, or overreaction that can destabilize positions and perception.

Recognizing feedback loops enables traders to **anticipate amplification or correction** and to manage risk and timing more effectively.

Superposition

Superposition, a concept adapted from quantum mechanics, describes the simultaneous existence of multiple potential outcomes or decisions until observation or action collapses the state. In trading, it refers to situations where **indecision, uncertainty, or multiple possibilities coexist**, and the trader's perception and choice determine which state manifests. Awareness of superposition helps in **embracing uncertainty as information** rather than paralysis.

Observer Effect

The observer effect highlights that the act of observing a system can influence its behavior. In trading, monitoring, analyzing, or participating in markets **affects price dynamics, sentiment, and probabilities**. Understanding this effect emphasizes that traders are **active participants**, not passive spectators, and that perception and action are inherently intertwined with market outcomes.

Flow

Flow is a mental and emotional state in which a trader's awareness, intuition, and action are fully aligned with market rhythms. In flow, decision-making becomes **effortless, precise, and timely**, enhancing sensitivity to micro-signals and resonance. Flow states are cultivated through practice, mindfulness, and alignment of mind and emotion.

Market Micro-Signals

Market micro-signals are subtle, often transient indicators of emerging trends or sentiment shifts. Examples include small price fluctuations, minor volume spikes, order book imbalances, and short-term behavioral patterns. Detecting these signals requires **attentive observation, emotional calibration, and contextual understanding**.

Psychological Market Inertia

Psychological market inertia refers to the tendency of market participants to **repeat behaviors or maintain sentiment trends** even after the initial catalysts have diminished. This inertia creates patterns, echo effects, and recurring cycles that can be leveraged for timing, trend recognition, and anticipation of corrections.

Emotional Calibration

Emotional calibration is the practice of recognizing, measuring, and aligning one's emotional state with market dynamics to optimize decision-making. It involves techniques such as mindfulness, reflection, journaling, and structured exercises that enhance **awareness, clarity, and flow**.

Co-Created Reality

Markets are a co-created reality, meaning price action, sentiment, and patterns emerge from the collective decisions, beliefs, and interactions of participants. Each trader **contributes to and is influenced by** this shared system, creating a dynamic interplay between individual agency and collective behavior.

Timing and Resonance

Timing and resonance refer to identifying the **optimal moments to act** in the market based on alignment between internal awareness, market micro-signals, and probabilistic assessment. Mastery of timing relies on observing emotional frequency, flow states, and subtle oscillations in sentiment.

> *"Mastery of markets begins with mastery of the concepts that govern perception, emotion, and action. Understanding these terms allows the trader to navigate complexity with clarity, resonance, and intentionality."*

Exercises

This appendix provides practical exercises designed to help traders **calibrate their emotions, strengthen perception, and enhance resonance with market dynamics**. These exercises translate the conceptual frameworks of this book into applied practice, enabling a deeper understanding of market behavior and personal alignment.

1. Emotional Calibration Drills

Emotional calibration is the process of recognizing, monitoring, and aligning your emotional state with market dynamics. These drills help develop sensitivity to subtle shifts in sentiment and maintain coherence during trading.

1. **Daily Emotional Check-In:** At the start of each trading session, spend 3–5 minutes noting your current emotional state. Use a scale from 1–10 for intensity and identify dominant emotions (e.g., calm, anxious, excited). Record these in a trading journal.

2. **Market Reflection Exercise:** After each trade or market session, reflect on how your emotions influenced your decisions. Identify moments where emotion enhanced or impaired judgment. Write a short summary of insights and adjustments.

3. **Micro-Signal Awareness:** Choose a single asset or market segment and focus on subtle price and volume movements. Note your intuitive feelings about potential shifts and compare them with actual outcomes to calibrate **emotional responsiveness**.

2. Pattern Silence Observation

Pattern silence observation trains the trader to **detect subtle signals and anticipate changes without over-interpreting noise**. This exercise emphasizes patience, observation, and heightened awareness.

1. **Silent Market Watching:** Choose a live chart or asset and observe for 5–10 minutes without placing trades. Focus on micro-fluctuations,

volume changes, or unusual patterns. Avoid making decisions; simply note observations.

2. **Emotion-Free Reflection:** After observation, write down what you noticed without judgment or analysis. Highlight patterns that stood out and any emotional reactions triggered. Repeat daily to strengthen **non-reactive observation**.

3. **Resonance Mapping:** Over several sessions, map recurring micro-patterns and your emotional responses to them. Identify **moments of natural resonance** where your intuition aligns with market behavior.

3. Flow and Timing Exercises

Flow and timing exercises help traders **synchronize attention, intuition, and action** with market rhythms to identify optimal entry and exit points.

1. **Flow Induction Routine:** Before trading, spend 5–10 minutes in a focused state breathing exercises, mindfulness, or visualization of market scenarios. Enter the session **fully present**, noting moments of heightened awareness and clarity.

2. **Peak Resonance Identification:** During live trading, record moments when your decisions feel effortless and aligned with market movement. Compare outcomes with these peak resonance points to refine **timing and pattern recognition**.

3. **Pause-and-Reflect Drill:** At any sign of emotional escalation or uncertainty, pause for 30–60 seconds. Assess whether action is aligned with flow or reactionary. Only proceed if resonance and coherence are restored.

4. **Session Review and Iteration:** After each trading day, review your flow states, emotional alignment, and timing decisions. Identify lessons, adjust routines, and plan exercises for the next session to enhance **continuous improvement**.

"Practice is not mastery, but mastery requires practice. These exercises are tools to refine perception, align action with flow, and build the subtle intuition necessary for resonant trading."

Case Studies

This appendix presents historical and contemporary market events analyzed through the lens of **resonance, emotional frequency, and collective behavior**. By examining these examples, traders can see how emotional energy, feedback loops, and market coherence influence price action, offering practical lessons for observation, timing, and alignment.

1. The Dot-Com Bubble (1995–2000)

Overview: The Dot-Com Bubble exemplifies how collective excitement and speculative behavior can amplify market trends. Rapid inflows of capital into technology stocks created a **constructive feedback loop**, increasing valuations independent of fundamental performance.

Resonance Analysis:

- **Emotional Frequency:** Extreme hope and optimism dominated the market, with fear largely absent until the final collapse.
- **Micro-Signals:** Early signs included disproportionate price movements relative to earnings and widespread narrative-driven investment.
- **Feedback Loops:** Positive reinforcement occurred as media hype and rising prices attracted more traders, magnifying emotional amplitude.

Lesson: Understanding emotional resonance can help identify **overheated markets** and the tipping point at which constructive loops turn destructive.

2. The 2008 Global Financial Crisis

Overview: Triggered by the collapse of the subprime mortgage market, the 2008 crisis illustrates how negative sentiment and misaligned leverage propagate through global markets.

Resonance Analysis:

- **Emotional Frequency:** Panic, fear, and distrust cascaded across sectors.

- **Market Memory:** Past bullish cycles contributed to underestimation of risk, creating **psychological inertia**.
- **Feedback Loops:** Forced deleveraging amplified market downturns, demonstrating a **destructive resonance loop**.

Lesson: Recognizing early **fear signals and systemic misalignments** can allow traders to adapt before crises escalate.

3. The Flash Crash (May 6, 2010)

Overview: The Flash Crash shows how microstructure and high-frequency trading can induce rapid market movements, even without fundamental news.

Resonance Analysis:

- **Micro-Oscillations:** Extreme price movements occurred in seconds due to algorithmic feedback loops.
- **Emotional Amplification:** Traders reacting to automated signals created secondary panic, demonstrating **emotional mirroring**.
- **Observation Effect:** Human observation and intervention eventually stabilized prices, collapsing superposed market states.

Lesson: Markets are sensitive to both human and automated feedback, highlighting the importance of **mindful observation and rapid response**.

4. Bitcoin Rally (2017–2018)

Overview: Bitcoin's explosive growth demonstrates how collective belief, narrative, and emotional energy create a **resonance-driven bubble** in a decentralized market.

Resonance Analysis:

- **Emotional Frequency:** Extreme greed and FOMO dominated, with new entrants amplifying the trend.
- **Pattern Recognition:** Recurrent cycles of hype and correction illustrate **macro- and micro-oscillations**.
- **Feedback Loops:** Social media and media coverage reinforced sentiment, creating high-amplitude movements.

Lesson: Monitoring collective cognition and narrative-driven resonance can guide **timing and risk modulation** in speculative markets.

5. S&P 500 Recovery Post-COVID-19 (2020)

Overview: Following the initial COVID-19 crash, the S&P 500 experienced a rapid rebound, demonstrating **constructive resonance between policy, investor confidence, and market perception.**

Resonance Analysis:

- **Emotional Frequency:** Fear quickly transitioned to hope and cautious optimism.
- **Flow Alignment:** Traders who aligned perception and action with market recovery captured high-probability opportunities.
- **Feedback Loops:** Fiscal stimulus and positive news reinforced upward momentum, illustrating **coherent amplification.**

Lesson: Recognizing transitions in **emotional waves and market rhythm** allows traders to participate in recovery without being driven by panic or greed.

"Case studies show that markets are not random; they are living, resonant systems influenced by collective emotion, perception, and feedback. Mastery comes from observing, feeling, and aligning with these patterns."

Suggested Reading

This appendix provides a curated list of books, research papers, and frameworks that complement the conceptual and practical approaches presented in this book. These resources cover **behavioral finance, psychology, mindfulness, and quantum decision theory**, helping traders deepen understanding of market dynamics and personal alignment.

1. Behavioral Finance

Behavioral finance explores how psychological factors influence investor behavior and market outcomes.

- **"Thinking, Fast and Slow" Daniel Kahneman** A foundational work on cognitive biases, heuristics, and dual-system thinking, offering insight into how human behavior shapes market dynamics.
- **"Misbehaving: The Making of Behavioral Economics" Richard H. Thaler** Explores the evolution of behavioral economics and provides case studies illustrating non-rational market behavior.
- **"Behavioral Finance: Psychology, Decision-Making, and Markets" Lucy Ackert and Richard Deaves** Offers academic and practical perspectives on how emotions, cognition, and social influences affect trading decisions.

2. Psychology and Cognitive Science

Understanding the mind, perception, and emotional regulation is crucial for resonant trading.

- **"Emotional Intelligence" Daniel Goleman** Explains the importance of self-awareness, self-regulation, and social awareness in professional and personal contexts.
- **"The Psychology of Trading" Brett N. Steenbarger** Focused on developing mental and emotional strategies to navigate markets, including exercises for self-reflection and flow.

- **"Thinking in Systems" Donella H. Meadows** Introduces systems thinking principles, helping traders understand feedback loops, emergent behavior, and market interconnectedness.

3. Mindfulness and Flow

Practices in mindfulness and flow states enhance perception, emotional stability, and decision-making alignment.

- **"Flow: The Psychology of Optimal Experience" Mihaly Csikszentmihalyi** Explains how to achieve flow states and maximize engagement, performance, and awareness.
- **"The Mindful Trader" David M. Gordon** Provides practical mindfulness exercises specifically tailored for trading and financial decision-making.
- **"Wherever You Go, There You Are" Jon Kabat-Zinn** Offers practical guidance on cultivating mindfulness and presence in daily life and professional environments.

4. Quantum Decision Theory and Conceptual Frameworks

These works explore the intersection of cognition, uncertainty, and probabilistic thinking.

- **"Quantum Finance: Path Integrals and Hamiltonians for Options and Interest Rates" Belal E. Baaquie** Introduces quantum concepts applied to financial modeling and uncertainty, linking probability and market dynamics.
- **"Quantum Social Science: Concepts and Applications" Emmanuel Haven and Andrei Khrennikov** Explores how quantum theory can model human cognition, decision-making, and collective behavior.
- **"The Principles of Quantum Mechanics" P.A.M. Dirac** While a physics text, its conceptual rigor and probabilistic thinking provide inspiration for understanding **superposition, uncertainty, and entanglement in markets**.

5. Integrative and Conceptual Works

These texts bridge multiple disciplines, offering frameworks for understanding markets as living, resonant systems.

- **"Antifragile: Things That Gain from Disorder" Nassim Nicholas Taleb** Discusses risk, uncertainty, and the dynamics of complex systems, emphasizing adaptive decision-making.
- **"The Wisdom of Crowds" James Surowiecki** Explores collective behavior, group cognition, and emergent intelligence in markets and social systems.
- **"Synchronicity: An Acausal Connecting Principle" Carl G. Jung** Conceptual work on meaningful coincidences and patterns, useful for understanding psychological resonance and narrative in trading.

"Reading across disciplines finance, psychology, mindfulness, and conceptual frameworks enables traders to cultivate a resonant mindset, perceive subtle market signals, and make aligned, coherent decisions."

References / Bibliography

This bibliography compiles key academic, professional, and conceptual sources referenced throughout the book, spanning behavioral finance, market psychology, decision theory, mindfulness, and complex systems. Readers can use these works for deeper study, verification, and application of the frameworks presented.

Behavioral Finance and Market Psychology

- Kahneman, D. (2011). *Thinking, Fast and Slow.* Farrar, Straus and Giroux.
- Thaler, R. H. (2015). *Misbehaving: The Making of Behavioral Economics.* W.W. Norton & Company.
- Ackert, L. F., & Deaves, R. (2010). *Behavioral Finance: Psychology, Decision-Making, and Markets.* South-Western Cengage Learning.
- Steenbarger, B. N. (2003). *The Psychology of Trading.* Wiley.
- Shefrin, H. (2000). *Beyond Greed and Fear: Understanding Behavioral Finance and the Psychology of Investing.* Harvard Business School Press.

Cognition, Mindfulness, and Flow

- Goleman, D. (1995). *Emotional Intelligence.* Bantam Books.
- Csikszentmihalyi, M. (1990). *Flow: The Psychology of Optimal Experience.* Harper & Row.
- Kabat-Zinn, J. (1994). *Wherever You Go, There You Are.* Hyperion.
- Gordon, D. M. (2010). *The Mindful Trader.* Wiley.

Complex Systems and Decision Theory

- Taleb, N. N. (2012). *Antifragile: Things That Gain from Disorder.* Random House.
- Surowiecki, J. (2004). *The Wisdom of Crowds.* Anchor Books.
- Meadows, D. H. (2008). *Thinking in Systems: A Primer.* Chelsea Green Publishing.
- Jung, C. G. (1973). *Synchronicity: An Acausal Connecting Principle.* Princeton University Press.

Quantum Decision and Finance

- Baaquie, B. E. (2007). *Quantum Finance: Path Integrals and Hamiltonians for Options and Interest Rates.* Cambridge University Press.
- Haven, E., & Khrennikov, A. (2013). *Quantum Social Science: Concepts and Applications.* Cambridge University Press.
- Dirac, P. A. M. (1981). *The Principles of Quantum Mechanics.* Oxford University Press.

Market Case Studies and Historical References

- Shiller, R. J. (2000). *Irrational Exuberance.* Princeton University Press.
- Lowenstein, R. (2000). *When Genius Failed: The Rise and Fall of Long-Term Capital Management.* Random House.
- Lewis, M. (2010). *The Big Short: Inside the Doomsday Machine.* W.W. Norton & Company.
- Yermack, D. (2018). *Corporate Governance and Blockchains.* Review of Finance, 22(1), 1–50.

Additional References

- Taleb, N. N. (2007). *The Black Swan: The Impact of the Highly Improbable.* Random House.
- Kahneman, D., Slovic, P., & Tversky, A. (1982). *Judgment Under Uncertainty: Heuristics and Biases.* Cambridge University Press.
- Fama, E. F., & French, K. R. (1993). *Common Risk Factors in the Returns on Stocks and Bonds.* Journal of Financial Economics, 33(1), 3–56.

"This collection of references reflects the multidisciplinary foundation of market resonance, integrating psychology, behavioral finance, complex systems, and quantum-inspired frameworks."

www.ingramcontent.com/pod-product-compliance
Lightning Source LLC
Chambersburg PA
CBHW050526240926
51846CB00003B/711
* 9 7 8 9 3 3 4 4 5 1 1 9 1 *